BACKYARD BEEKEEPERS
OF THE BAY AREA

BY JUDITH ADAMSON

ILLUSTRATIONS BY LISA ADAMSON

Backyard Beekeepers of the Bay Area
By Judith Adamson
Illustrations by Lisa Adamson

Copyright 2011 by Slanted Light Press,
An imprint of Speed Bump Press
7523 Fairmount Avenue
El Cerrito, CA 94530
www.backyardbeekeepersbayarea.com

All Rights Reserved

No part of this book may be reproduced or transmitted in any form or by any means, electronic or mechanical, including photocopying, recording, or by any information storage and retrieval system, without the written consent of the publisher.

Publisher's Cataloguing-in-Publication Data

Adamson, Judith 1949-
    Backyard Beekeepers of the Bay Area /Judith   Adamson
      Paperback ISBN-13: 978-0-9762362-3-8
      p. cm.
Illustrations by Lisa Adamson 1947-

Ebook ISBN-13: 978-0-9762362-6-9

Adamson, Judith
 1. Honeybees — California --San Francisco Bay Area. 2. Beekeeping

SF524.52.C2.A43 2011
638.1 — dc22

Printed and bound in the United States of America
10 9 8 7 6 5 4 3 2 1 / 14 13 12 11 10

To My Sisters:
Lisa, Star and Kath

CONTENTS

1 AN UNEASY SILENCE	1
2 IN GRATITUDE FOR THE HONEYBEE	7
3 SOCIAL COHESION	15
4 HONEY ROBBERS TO BEEKEEPERS	27
5 THE BEEKEEPERS	32

The Rogue Beekeeper, David Eichorn	33
Perfumer & Beekeeper, Laurie Stern	39
Floral Designer & Beekeeper, Patricia Gibbons	46
The Beekeeping Gene, Steve Gentry	50
The Philosopher Beekeeper, Eli Waddle	58
The Patient Beekeeper, Leah Fortin	63
Accidental Beekeepers, Pia & Jim Williams	70
The Johnny Appleseed of Honeybees, Bill Tomaszewski	73
Google: The Engineer Beekeeper, Rob Peterson	78
Google: The Chef Beekeeper, Marc Rasic	81
Google: The Physicist Beekeeper, Greg Robinson	84
The Beekeeper & the Beekeeper's Wife, Spencer & Helene Marshall	87
The Honeybees of Nob Hill, Fairmont Hotel's Chef JW Foster	92
Our Pollen Princesses, Michael Cooper & Deno Marcum	98
The Lost Art of Bee Tracking, Tom Manger	104
First Swarm, Bill Hoskins	108

Urban Farmer & Beekeeper, Mauro Correa   110
The Great Sunflower Project, Gretchen LeBuhn   116
The Observant Beekeeper, Prodromos Stephanos   121
The Melissa Garden, Barbara Shlumberger   127
A Different Kind of Beekeeper, Michael Thiele   131

6 CONCENTRATED GOODNESS   143
7 GARDEN NOTES: WE NEED ALL THE
       POLLINATORS WE CAN GET   151
8 BEEKEEPERS' FAVORITE RECIPES   159

RESOURCES   175

1
AN UNEASY SILENCE

Much more than we can imagine depends on the
presence and vitality of the honeybee population.
-Gunther Hauk

AN UNEASY SILENCE

Solitary bees flourished over a hundred and twenty million years ago when Tyrannosaurus Rex was still roaming Earth. Sixty-five million years ago the tiny bees managed to survive the catastrophic event that caused the sudden mass extinction of most of the other species on earth; thirty five million years ago a few solitary bees veered onto an evolutionary detour to become the social honeybee we know today. Man, depending on one's definition of human, emerged anywhere from a mere two hundred sixty thousand to thirty thousand years ago. Compared to the bees, we've just arrived.

Co-evolving alongside bees were flowering plants, and the flower and the bee began to shape a spectacularly ingenious symbiotic partnership. Flowers, the reproductive organs of plants, contain both the male and female parts, and it is their biological function to bring about the union of male sperm with female ovum to produce fertilized seeds. Plants release dust-like pollen—the cells that carry male DNA—into the air and this pollen must *somehow* make its journey down the sticky bulb—the stigma—protruding from the center of the flower into the female part, which contains the precious seeds. When pollen meets ovary, fertilization takes place, and the fruit begins to swell.

Over millions of years, flowers have developed an astonishing array of strategies to attract the attention of the partners they needed to transport pollen to stigma. Not only did they develop a substance with an alluring scent and taste —nectar—they also fashioned themselves into showy displays of different designs, colors and shapes. Amazingly, pollinators evolved simultaneously to fit the flowers! Some grew long noses, some long tongues, some developed hairy legs, others developed vision that could only see red, some could see ultraviolet, others preferred a musky smell. It was, and still is, an ingenious symbiotic relationship, a solution to what could have been a major evolutionary glitch.

Nowhere is this co-evolution more inspired than that between the flower and the honeybee, which have developed over eons to fulfill each other's needs. Their partnership is so intertwined that extinction of one would devastate the other.

Sugary sweet nectar lies deep inside the flower and entices the honeybee to come drink. She lands on the petals of the blossom, guided by designs only she can see, seduced by the promise of nectar and pollen. A narrow tube leading to the nectar fits the length of her straw-like tongue, and as she sips, pollen clings to the hairs on her body like a fuzzy aura. She moves to the next blossom, and as she dives to drink the nectar, little grains of pollen are pulled off her body by the sticky stamen of the flower. This facilitates the crucial meeting of floral sperm and ovum ... which insures fertilization... which forms the fruit... which contains the seeds to create the next generation of flowering plant... which entices the honeybee to come drink its sweet nectar and gather its pollen. This fleeting moment, simultaneously purposeful and inadvertent, has provided the honeybee with food and the flower with progeny. The relationship between the flower and the bee has been a completely sustainable loop for many millions of years.

At first, humans slipped gracefully into this seemingly never-ending loop, reaping the benefits of the partnership between the flower and the bee—a bountiful harvest—but over time, greed and misuse have disrupted this harmonious cycle, unraveling such sustainable perfection.

Honeybees are an indispensable but increasingly fragile part of our ecosystem, playing an essential role not only in the natural world but in the human world as well. They pollinate at least one-third of the fruits and vegetables we humans eat. They pollinate plants that wild animals eat and also crops like alfalfa and clover, which feed the animals who supply us with meat and dairy. Honeybees are our primary pollinators and inadvertently give us the extraordinary gift of their surplus honey. Without them, much of what we have would rapidly cease to exist, and we'd return to a lackluster diet of wind-pollinated wheat, corn and rice.

Of the pollinators—bees, bats, hummingbirds, butterflies and moths (all of whom are in peril)—only honeybees can be "managed" by humans. This makes them the most efficient of all the pollinators because they live in colonies and can be moved and concentrated when and where needed. Recently, however, something alarming has been happening. Several years ago, commercial beekeepers began to notice a startling decline in their honeybee populations. An uneasy silence replaced the industrious hum of their bees, and when checking on their hives, beekeepers often saw the queen but very few workers. Most shocking, however, was the capped honeycomb with baby bees still snug in their cells. Honeybees do not abandon their young, and it appeared that workers had flown out of the hive and simply not returned.

Neatly tagged as a "disorder," this recurring event is known as Colony Collapse Disorder and has entomologists, biologists, agriculturalists and apiarists stymied. There are many theories—mites, pesticide exposure, antibiotics, cell towers, the trucking of bees for long distances, inadequate food supply, genetically modified plants, a virulent new virus, mono-crop farming and mono-orchards that have replaced natural diversity—but the cause remains a mystery and a sinister foreshadowing of things to come. In 1923, Rudolf Steiner predicted that within eighty to a hundred years commercial beekeeping would annihilate the honeybee. We are disturbingly on schedule. It is estimated that well over half of all honeybee colonies in the United States have disappeared in the last few years. Their demise reaches far into our fields and orchards and from there onto our dinner tables.

Once the honeybee was revered. In many cultures she symbolized the soul, was emulated as the Great Mother, thought of as divine, a goddess. She stood for social order and community generosity. She was venerated for her ability to produce wax, which provided light, and honey, considered sacred because of its curative powers.

In modern times the honeybee has been taken for granted as a cog in the wheel of industrialized beekeeping. There is intense concern about how many mono crops honeybees can pollinate, how much honey can be taken from their hives and how much money will be generated. Apiaries have become factories; bees are fed sugar water so more honey can be taken from them; they are given chemicals to kill bloodsucking Varroa mites which prey on the weakened bees; queens are artificially inseminated; hundreds of colonies are trucked all over the country to land in unfamiliar places. Honeybees are treated as poorly and impersonally as cows or chickens on factory farms.

California has the largest beekeeping industry of any state in the United States. There are not enough bees in the state to pollinate the almond trees, a huge industry for California, so they must be trucked in from all over the country. Industrial beekeeping on such a huge, fast moving scale cannot possibly be beneficial for honeybees, as millions, traveling on flatbeds at 75 mph, cling precariously to their queen by fragile pheromones clouded by toxic fumes.

Only by understanding the nature of the honeybee and working *with* her natural instincts and rhythms, not exploiting those instincts, can we attempt to restore her strength. Does the key to saving the honeybee, perhaps, lie in the hives of backyard beekeepers?

Beekeepers with only a hive or two can treat the destructive Varroa mite organically. They can place the hives in areas that protect them from harsh weather and predators, and give them a stable place from which to set out to forage. Being guardians—not entrepreneurs—they will take only the honey that is indeed surplus and not a drop more.

As Colony Collapse Disorder reaches farther into the consciousness of the Bay Area, more people are slipping on the veil and bee suit. Those not predisposed to beekeeping can encourage and support our local beekeepers. In addition, we can plant bee-friendly—indeed, all-pollinator-friendly—gardens to reestablish dwindling forage areas. There couldn't be a better place than the Bay Area for backyard beekeeping, individual and community gardens and orchards. We have the yards, there's always something blooming, and we have a population committed to preserving the natural beauty and ecology of the area.

In return for offering sanctuary for a colony or two, the backyard beekeeper reaps the benefit of a lush garden (as does his/her neighbors), fruit bearing trees, a little honey, the privilege of witnessing the endless mysteries of the honeybee, and the honor of entering a sustainable loop where nothing is wasted and nothing harmed.

2
IN GRATITUDE
FOR THE HONEYBEE

When California was wild, it was one sweet
bee-garden throughout its entire length,
north and south, and all the way across
from the snowy Sierra to the ocean.
-John Muir

IN GRATITUDE FOR THE HONEYBEE

The Bay Area, in its wild, uncharted beauty, must have been breathtaking when inhabited by the Ohlone. The indigenous people flourished here for over three thousand years when tule grasses grew in the marshlands, and oak and redwood covered the hills. They hunted game, caught abundant fish in the bay and the Pacific, gathered berries and seeds and harvested acorns to grind into flour for bread.

Zealous Spanish missionaries, determined to convert the unsuspecting Ohlone to Catholicism, settled Mission Dolores in San Francisco, bringing with them orchard and garden seeds from the Old World to feed the mission. The Franciscan padres planted oranges, figs, olives, grapes and vegetables but soon realized the peninsula's damp, foggy climate was inadequate for gardening and lacked space for grazing. They sent their cattle and sheep across the bay to graze on the sweet grasses that grew where the Ohlone had lived so long, now claimed for the king of Spain. Planting gardens on the warmer side of the bay, they enslaved the Ohlone on their own land and introduced diseases that eventually decimated them.

Over two thousand species of wild, solitary bees had inhabited the area from the time native flowers took root millions of years ago. Honeybees, however, were not native to the area. It is believed that Russian settlers carried them across the Bering Strait to Alaska in the early 1800s and down into California, but few survived. They arrived more successfully from the east. Having originated in Africa, they spread to Asia and Europe; from there settlers brought bee colonies from England to Virginia and Massachusetts in the early 1600s. They thrived in the colonies, providing wax for candles and honey for sweetener and medicinal purposes.

As settlers expanded west across the United States, they carried their beehives with them, and swarms settled into feral colonies that spread as far as the Great Plains. Appalled Native Americans dreaded the imminent approach of settlers when they saw masses of "the white man's flies" arriving. Unable to cross the Rockies on their own, honeybees were often shipped from the eastern states to Panama, taken across the isthmus and shipped up the coast to California. In 1853 Christopher Shelton bought twelve hives in Panama, carried them by rail, mule and steamer to San Francisco and launched an apiary near San Jose. Only one colony survived, but it produced major swarms; probably many of the Bay Area's current honeybees are descended from those swarms.

The Gold Rush of the mid 1800s brought a flood of fortune-hunters, eager to pan a pot of gold, to northern California, and San Francisco grew rapidly from tent town to boom town. This first influx was followed by others over the next hundred years as the promise of riches and opportunity drew people to this exciting new frontier. Cultural diversity brought botanical diversity as new plants and gardening techniques were introduced from other countries and other parts of the United States.

John Muir, the impassioned naturalist who wandered from the Sierras to the Pacific at the end of the 19th Century, was enthralled by California, calling it "one sweet bee-garden" with something blooming year round. But he also lamented that "of late, plows and sheep have made sad havoc in these glorious pastures..." and predicted the time when "flowers would vanish in ever-widening circles" and with them, presumably, the bee.

  Settlement of the East Bay began at the water's edge and moved gradually towards the hills as the population grew. Old photos show homesteads with fruit trees and gardens enclosed by picket fences, surrounded by open grazing land. One can imagine honeybees busily pollinating fruits and vegetables for the kitchen and clover for grazing cattle. Redwoods were cut from the hills for timber, and to re-tree quickly, fast-growing eucalyptus were introduced. The clusters of white flowers on this lofty tree became a favorite of the honeybee.

  As San Francisco reeled from the earthquake of 1906, the population of the East Bay grew by leaps and bounds with city folk seeking safer ground. People embraced Craftsman-style bungalows, which gracefully integrated home interiors with the ubiquitous beauty of nature. Porches opened onto flower and vegetable gardens, and fruit trees stood within arms' reach of the kitchen. The Bay Area's love affair with anything growing was in full bloom.

***

  Today the Bay Area is still remarkably beautiful despite the clumsy footprint of human civilization. Its magnificent topography surrounds us on a grand scale—the expanse of the jade-tinted Bay, the Golden Gate, the wild Marin Headlands and the gentle hills of the East Bay. We live in this beauty on a personal scale also—back yards and roof gardens, tree-lined streets, flowers anyplace there's a patch to grow something. For such natural beauty to be so accessible to everyone in a major urban area is unique.

The East Bay Hills, like a giant amphitheater overlooking San Francisco Bay, run for fifteen miles from Richmond south through Oakland. How fortunate that some ancient crash of tectonic plates pushed up these hills, allowing spectacular, unobstructed views of the Bay from the many houses that step down the hills. With bright western exposure, refreshing breezes off the Bay and front row seats to magnificent sunsets, there's a feeling of removal from urban commotion, yet access to city life is only minutes away.

Most plots in the hills provide ample front and back yards, perfect for planting. The hills slope gently into a plain that runs to the bay. Houses here in the "flats" feel less rural, but the yards, laid out by early settlers to accommodate their kitchen gardens, are often large enough to grow a small vegetable garden or sustain several fruit trees.

The Bay Area's climate is considered Mediterranean with winters generally cool and wet and summers hot and dry. San Francisco, however, can be downright bone-chilling in summer. Moisture-filled air pulled from the frigid Pacific by inland heat creates fog that rushes through the Golden Gate and lingers all day in the city, while across the Bay it burns off by mid morning leaving a dewy residue of moisture to nourish plants.

Given the flats and folds of the Bay Area's landscape, different micro-climates can exist in the same neighborhood, making botanical variety interesting. It seems just about anything grows here; in fact plants that grow all over the country and the world have taken deep root in the Bay Area. Apple and pear trees that thrive in the changing seasons of upstate New York or Wisconsin seem equally at home here. Lavender that fills the fields of Provence loves a nice sunny yard in the East Bay, and sage grows as happily here as it does in the high deserts of New Mexico.

IN GRATITUDE FOR THE HONEYBEE

Fruit trees line sidewalks and grace yards. Lemon, orange, and grapefruit trees bear fruit year round; in spring, apple, plum, pear, cherry, apricot, nectarine, peach, fig, persimmon, pomegranate and avocado blossom and, with proper pollination, produce bushels of fruit. Even one backyard fruit tree, if pollinated, can provide a surprising amount of fruit. Vines loaded with berries grow abundantly, and vegetables and herbs can be gathered right outside the door for the evening's meal. Many flowers, available only from a florist throughout the rest of the country grow here in sunny spots, from the flats of Oakland to the hills of Richmond to San Francisco's rooftop gardens.

From November to February there's (hopefully) much-needed rain, and by the end of January, when East Coast bees still have three frigid months to hunker down in their hives, Bay Area bees are ready to forage for nectar and pollen. When buds begin to show on the cherry trees, that's the signal for beekeepers to put extra boxes or "supers" on their hives in anticipation of the honey flow. By Valentine's Day a spectacular show of cherry blossoms entices the bees to come gather nectar and pollen, and a new season of honey making has begun.

***

None of this vast array of botanical life would last very long if it weren't for honeybees and other pollinators who perpetuate the beauty and insure the survival of so many plants. We take them for granted—bees, bats, beetles, hummingbirds, moths, butterflies—and as urban development of our human habitat expands, their habitats drastically dwindle. Our intrusion has toppled the balance that once existed. One tiny hummingbird needs to drink the nectar from between a thousand to two thousand flowers each day, but urban sprawl over the country has destroyed areas that once had many nectar-producing flowers, diminishing stops across the birds' migration routes. Only a few species of bat are found in the Bay Area where many once thrived. As human development over the last hundred years has forever altered the landscape, bats are loosing their natural roosting sites, and the woodlands where they fed have been destroyed. Human invasion of habitat has eradicated many native plants that moths and butterflies depend on for food.

Of the two thousand species of native Californian bees, only *eighty* have been spotted in San Francisco recently, and their numbers are declining. They are solitary bees who don't produce honey but are major pollinators of fruits, nuts, vegetables and wildflowers. As suburbia spreads, their options shrink. Fields of wildflowers, which have intricately co-evolved with native bees over millions of years, are plowed under to make room for the next shopping mall or housing development.

The most prolific of the pollinators is the honeybee. Until recently, she lived on this planet in a gracefully sustainable partnership with flowers, never needing humans for her survival. We, on the other hand, have *always* needed the honeybee for our survival. Now, because of our exploitative, insensitive and irreverent ways, the honeybee is in grave danger. It is time to rekindle our reverence. Such respect can only come from an understanding of her nature, a recognition of the profound service she provides the planet, and an unwillingness to exploit her further. The honeybee is intriguing and mysterious, as we'll hear from some of the backyard beekeepers of the Bay Area, who invariably say that the more they learn, the less they know about these amazing creatures.

Welcome to the dazzling world of the honeybee.

3
SOCIAL COHESION

In order to do justice to an animal—and as human beings this is, or should be, a moral obligation—we must have a deep understanding of its nature. We cannot simply consider our own comfort and calculate our economic situation. If we do, we will face dire consequences.
           -Rudolf Steiner

SOCIAL COHESION

A Colony is Born

Only the bees know the tipping point when it's time for half the hive to leave to create a new colony. For the beekeeper, a telltale sign of imminent swarming is a cluster of bees hanging from the hive entrance on a warm day, but the bees have been preparing for some time. As the colony approaches swarming size, the workers create several queen cells, which are larger, peanut-shaped, and hang vertically. They move a recently fertilized egg into each of these cells and fill the cells with nutrient-rich royal jelly to feed the larvae. The first of these queens to emerge stings the other cells to kill any competition. When it is certain the daughter queen is firmly in place, the mother queen initiates the swarm, leaving with half the hive to establish a new colony.

The swarm clusters on a branch or in a shrub—thousands of bees linked together surrounding and protecting their queen. Having gorged on honey before leaving the old hive in preparation for the days it will take to find their new home, their full bellies pacify them and reduce their ability to sting. They are less defensive since they are not in their own hive with brood and food to protect. The huge mass may remain for several days while scouts search for suitable locations for a new home.

Several scout bees explore far and wide for possible new homes, analyzing the sites carefully for certain specifications. The cavity must be large enough to hold their winter honey supply; it must be high enough to discourage predators; the entrance must be only about an inch in diameter; and the site must face south for warmth.

When they return to the swarm, they perform the Waggle Dance on the surface of the swarm to communicate the location of the potential site and their enthusiasm for it. The more vigorous dancers elicit support and gain recruits to go look at the various sites. Less enthusiastic dancers lose supporters. If a bee who has gone to check out a suggested spot agrees it is a good choice, she also dances to recommend it. Gradually, excitement for less favorable locations dwindles, as dancers switch allegiance and begin dancing for the preferred sites. This can go on for several days and nights. At night they communicate direction by dancing at an angle related to the sun *on the other side of the earth!* Gradually a consensus builds among the scouts, and when a quorum congregates at one site, a decision has been made. The scouts return again to the swarm, clamber quickly through the huddled mass, and touching their buzzing thoraxes against the waiting bees in a kind of benediction, signal them to warm up their wing muscles and prepare for flight. When the entire swarm has warmed to 98 degrees, it lifts and departs for its new home and a new colony is born.

Geometry of the Hive

Honeybees live in colonies ranging from 20,000 to over 60,000 bees. Their hive is an architectural masterpiece and an engineering marvel. Whether in a tree hollow in the wild or on the frames of a man-made hive, form and function unite at their purest in the honeycomb. An elegant structure built from many hexagonally-shaped cells made from millions of minute flakes of wax are laid in place by hundreds of bees with absolute precision.

It is unsure how they accomplish this feat of engineering, but observation makes the process look like this: Con-

SOCIAL COHESION

struction starts at the top in several places at once. At twelve to fifteen days old, bees develop special glands capable of converting honey to wax. The young workers gorge on honey and when the little wax flakes seep through pores in their abdomen they mix them with saliva and knead them to a malleable consistency. Hanging in festoons—chains of bees interlinked by their legs—they pass the flakes from bee to bee until they reach the comb builders. Layers of wax are placed at the base and gradually the comb builders appear to draw out the cells by pulling and thinning the wax into walls using their legs and mandibles. The precision is remarkable with the angle between adjacent walls an exact 120 degrees. While the comb builders work, other bees cluster around providing body warmth to keep the wax from stiffening and becoming brittle. As a new bee joins the construction crew, she immediately understands the stage of the building and carries on, contributing to whatever task is needed for that cell. Although the cells are constructed in a piecemeal manner at two or three different sites simultaneously, ultimately each section is seamlessly linked with the others.

Each cell, which will become either a private compartment for a developing larva or storage for honey or pollen, slopes slightly upward so neither egg nor honey can spill out before it's capped. Shortly after each cell is completed, the warming crowd moves away, allowing the wax to harden to such a strength that ultimately the comb will be able to hold twenty pounds of honey for each pound of wax.

Among the possible geometric forms that might be suitable to the construction of the honeycomb—the square, triangle or hexagon—honeybees "chose" the hexagon. Over 1700 years ago, Pappus, the Alexandrian mathematician, proposed that bees not only had a divine sense of symmetry, but also a high degree of mathematical judgment in their choice of a hexagonal shape, since it required the least amount of material to hold the greatest amount of substance.

This led mathematicians to contemplate and attempt to prove what became known as the Hexagonal Honeycomb Conjecture, which theorized the most efficient way to partition a plane into equal areas was through the use of hexagons. Proof of this theory eluded mathematicians for seventeen centuries and was finally proven in 2008. Honeybees seem to have known this for millions of years. Not only does the hexagon use less wax than the triangle or the square, the three-dimensional hexagonal cells fit together neatly, creating the maximum amount of space using the least amount of wax and the most efficient expenditure of labor. According to engineers, it is the strongest shape for distributing load and handling forces of that load. Today "honeycomb" construction is used for bridges and airplane wings.

The geometrical perfection of the honeycomb threw a potential monkey-wrench into Charles Darwin's theory of evolution. He was not without wonder at their hives, and even *he* asked how something so complex could be engineered instinctively without the unmentionable—divine guidance. He even acknowledged it as a "difficulty sufficient to overthrow my whole theory." He concluded, however, (perhaps skirting the real question), that honeycomb is a masterpiece of engineering, but that the bees had no idea about angles or prisms or rhombic plates; they were merely building according to the motivation to economize wax. With that, he seemed to feel he was able to prove a key point and complete *On the Origin of Species by Means of Natural Selection.*

In man-made frame hives, the combs are orderly, dictated by the rectangular boundaries of the frames. Natural honeycomb built in the wild, however, is undulant, resembling a series of hanging lungs or the underside of a giant mushroom, which bees adjust to the cavity in which it's built. It falls in parallel sheets anchored to the roof of the cavity, each sheet approximately an inch thick, made of perfect hexagonal cells sitting back to back. The sheets hang as wide and as long as the cavity will allow and end in the gentle curve of a parabola, giving it added strength. When a natural obstacle is met, the sheet may curve slightly or turn a rounded corner. Burr-comb, which is crude and angled, attaches the numerous sheets to the interior of the cavity like flying buttresses, yet space between the sheets form the perfect-sized corridor for bees to maneuver throughout the comb.

The hexagonal cells are created in two sizes according to whether they will accommodate workers or drones. The majority of cells are for worker bees—smaller and built in the center of the hive where it is warmer. Larger drone cells are formed on the periphery, vulnerable to predators and drops in temperature, perhaps because drone brood is more expendable. The bees in their engineering wisdom store their honey in the upper part of the comb, close to the points of attachment in order to handle the heavy load.

Unfilled honeycomb is striking in its weightlessness. That such a seemingly delicate structure can hold a substance as dense and heavy as honey, is an engineering marvel.

The Queen

The queen—the one fertile female—is the mother of all bees in the hive and is solely responsible for bringing into being the next generation. It is her particular scent, or pheromone, that creates the social cohesion of a particular hive. The queen, unable to feed herself, is constantly attended by a ring of worker bees who feed her, give her water, clean and protect her.

When the hive becomes crowded, she conducts a swarm and leaves with half the bees, bequeathing the old hive to a daughter who has been fed royal jelly in a large cell in order to become the new queen. The virgin queen takes a series of grand matrimonial flights during which drones from different hives compete for her. She mates with several on each flight, insuring genetic diversity, and accumulates enough sperm for her lifetime, which is around three to six years. She spends her post-coital life laying up to 2,000 eggs a day, a necessity since her children only live a few months. Long and elegant, she moves methodically around the brood chamber, placing each egg, the size of a dot, gently into a cell according to the needs of the hive — an unfertilized egg from which a drone will emerge or a fertilized egg from which a worker will emerge.

The Drone

All drones are males and there are only several hundred per hive. Since a drone develops from an unfertilized egg, he does not have a father, only a grandfather, which assures his proper contribution to the gene pool. He does not forage or work in the hive and is unable to feed himself. His only job is to mate with a virgin queen from another hive, made more likely because he drifts from hive to hive. In the warm spring afternoons he flies out to a drone congregating area where he waits among his competitors until, with enormous eyes that cover most of his head, he spots a virgin queen. He is round and wide, but despite his girth, is capable of flying like a fuzzy bullet — as fast as the virgin queen. As he takes to the air with hundreds of other eager drones, the queen flies higher and higher. Weaker drones drop behind, but those who can keep up with her earn a chance to mate in mid-flight. The few who succeed in their life purpose are rewarded by death as their lower half is wrenched violently from their body, and the other half falls to the ground. After mating season is over, the other drones die as well, as the workers, no longer needing their services, drag them from the hive. Incapable of fending for themselves, they starve to an ignominious death.

SOCIAL COHESION

Sisterhood of the Worker Bees

A worker, although she comes from a fertilized egg, is infertile, so there can be no competition with the queen. She is a sister to every other worker because they share the same mother. Since the queen has mated with several drones, a worker can share three fourths of her genes with her super-sisters (same father) or fewer genes with her half sisters (different father). Perhaps it is this genetic closeness that fosters her generosity and altruism for her siblings and is a major reason why all work for the good of the whole. If she is hard pressed to sting in order to defend her community, perhaps it is this sibling bond that makes the suicidal act so natural.

A worker's stinger is actually her defunct, modified egg-laying apparatus with the added zing of a venom gland. When she emerges from her cell, metamorphosed from egg to larva to silk-enshrouded pupa to adult, she immediately becomes a house bee, her work confined to the hive for the first three weeks. Her first task is to clean cells of any debris. Gradually she moves into nurse bee, feeding the larvae, then into processing and storing the nectar and pollen, constructing the comb and guarding the entrance. Other in-house duties include attending the queen, feeding the drones, fanning the hive, removing dead bees, shoring up cracks in the hive. At three weeks, her duties in the hive done, she becomes a field bee and takes to the skies. From now until the end of her life when her wings have become tattered and torn, she'll spend her time gathering nectar, pollen, water and resin.

A worker has five eyes (some with hairs protruding), two stomachs, rotating antennae, hairy legs, buckets on her hind legs, a stinger, wax coming out of her abdomen, a spoon at the tip of her proboscis and nerve ganglia that processes information at 90,000 miles an hour.

Two humongous eyes, each with 6,000 hexagonal facets, take up most of her head. Each facet is like a little eye unto itself with its own lens able to capture light from a narrow angle of view. Three simpler eyes sit between the compound ones and sharpen her vision, letting in more light and helping her see better when she leaves the hive at dawn and returns at dusk. Her visual field is 360 degrees. At one end of the spectrum she can see ultraviolet light which enables her to perceive patterns on flowers that act like landing strips or bulls' eyes pointing to the nectar source. She sees rapid movement — 300 images a second (ten times more than humans) — so as she flies over a patch of blossoms they appear to twinkle as petals flutter to catch her attention. She can also detect polarized light, which allows her to "see" the sun through thick clouds. As if this weren't enough, hairs sticking out of her lenses measure the speed of the wind.

Her antennae, set in sockets that allow them to rotate freely, scan constantly for odors. She smells in stereo, each antenna ending in two noses. One hundred times more sensitive than a bloodhound's nose, they allow her to smell a nectar source far away. Through her antennae she can also hear, taste and touch, measure flight speed, take the temperature of the hive and measure carbon dioxide levels.

Her small, but sophisticated brain has large nerves that connect her antennae to her brain so it receives constant sensory input. Comparatively large areas of her brain also receive information from her eyes. Everything is stored in memory and called upon for countless complex behaviours, including a remarkable ability to learn.

The Waggle Dance and The Round Dance

A scout sets out on reconnaissance to find the richest source of nectar available and returns to tell the others. She enters the hive excitedly and heads for the dance floor. Here, on the vertical plane of the comb she must communicate horizontal direction. As her sisters gather round, she performs the Waggle Dance, shaking her butt and buzzing, going forward on a straight vector, which corresponds to the direction of the nectar source in relation to the sun. She loops to the right, returning to the starting point where she again dances forward on the vector, then loops to the left and back to the starting point. The intensity and duration of the waggle — the richer the source, the more energetic the dance — tells the others how far the flowers are. One hundred or more circuits tells them *exactly* the direction and distance of the source.

The honeybee, with a brain the size of a pinhead, has retained the information she gathered when seeking the nectar source, and has transposed the angle of the sun when she was flying to a gravitational angle. If the sun was 30 degrees to her left when she was flying towards the nectar, the wagging part of her dance will be on a 30 degree vector clockwise. During the time it takes her to perform the dance to communicate the location of the flowers and recruit her sisters, the position of the sun will have changed a few degrees and *she adjusts the vector of her dance accordingly*! During the dance, any bee may, with a squeaking sound, ask her to pause and give them a taste of the nectar, which she carries in her stomach.

When the nectar source is close by, within approximately 35 yards, she does a lower key dance called the Round Dance. She dances in a small circle one way and then changes direction describing a circle in the opposite direction. As if in a kind of conga line, numerous bees follow her closely, imitating her dance and getting a whiff of the flowers from which she drank the nectar. They know the food is close to the hive and what it smells like. With this information, they set off flying in ever widening circles to find the source.

Working the Bloom

Whether the source is near or far, the workers — pollen buckets at the ready — set out eagerly to work the blooms. Experts at time management, they go to only one kind of flower at a time; the more blossoms, the less time wasted in flitting from plant to plant. A by-product of being efficient, this focus ultimately intensifies the flavor of the honey.

The bee, drawn to the heady scent of nectar, sucks it from the flowers and stores it in her "honey stomach," a second stomach devoted solely to holding nectar. Hairs all over her body form an electromagnetic field and the pollen practically jumps off the flower's anthers onto her. Thin sacks, or pollen baskets, on her back legs expand as she rakes thousands of tiny grains of precious pollen into them, packing them tightly to haul back to the hive. In the process, grains of pollen are deposited onto the flower's stigma, starting their journey to fertilize the flower's seeds. The bee leaves a temporary scent on each flower she's visited to alert her sisters that she's already taken the nectar from that flower and not to waste their time. In an hour the scent will be gone, just enough time for the flower to refill with nectar.

Receiver Bees

Honey stomach full and pollen buckets loaded, the bee navigates back to the hive with her cargo. There she's met by receiver bees who suck the nectar from her stomach and transfer the pollen from her baskets into the comb to feed the baby bees. Nectar mixed with pollen is fed as beebread to the babies. If the field bee senses a delay in having her cargo unloaded because there are not enough receiver bees, she may perform the Tremble Dance to alert the hive that some of her sisters need to stop what they're doing and come help her unload so she can go forage again.

Alchemy

Receiver bees take the nectar and chew it for half an hour, adding enzymes, which break complex sugars into simple ones, making the nectar more digestible and less apt to be attacked by bacteria while being stored in the hive. They place it into cells throughout the honeycomb. The nectar is 80% water and will not become honey until the water has evaporated to 18%. Like chefs creating a reduction, the house bees fan the comb with their wings, hastening the evaporation process until the nectar distills to its essence, becoming honey. When thick enough, it's sealed into the cells with plugs of wax, available for the lean times of winter.

Temperature Control

During the hot months, the temperature of the hive must be maintained at about 98 degrees, just about the temperature of the human body. Water-carrying bees bring water back to the hive and spread it on the bottom where fanning bees help it evaporate to cool the nest.

During cooler times, as temperatures outside the hive drop, the bees cluster together to maintain heat. At the center is the queen, warm and protected. Those on the outermost edges pack together densely to form an insulation layer. Outer and inner bees switch positions regularly to keep warm, but the queen always remains in the center. She cannot get too cold or she will become infertile and unable to lay eggs in the spring—death to the hive. The cluster expands and contracts with the rising or falling temperature, and the entire mass moves slowly along the honeycomb, eating from the stores put up for winter.

Hopefully, the queen and her daughters winter-over successfully, and when the rains have stopped and cherry blossoms bloom in the Bay Area, the bees set out to follow the nectar flow once again.

4
HONEY ROBBERS
TO BEEKEEPERS

The keeping of bees is like trying to direct sunbeams.
-Henry David Thoreau

HONEY ROBBERS TO BEEKEEPERS

Our hominid ancestors were most likely plunging their hairy hands into beehives millions of years ago, but the earliest tangible record of honey harvesting appears on rock paintings from 7000 BC. Honey pilfered from hives has been used as food, currency, ritual offerings, a preservative for food and embalming, an aphrodisiac, a fertility enhancer, cosmetics and for medicinal purposes. Cupid dunked his arrows into the golden substance before shooting them into lovers. The gods of Mount Olympus knew it as ambrosia and became intoxicated on an alcoholic drink they made from it. Ancients revered honeybees because of their seemingly mystical ability to make honey. Honey is mentioned in the Hittite code, the sacred writings of India and Egypt, the Old Testament and the Koran. Early Romans considered it divine, calling it the "nectar of the gods." Hippocrates praised honey for its nutritional and medicinal value and it was discussed in the philosophical texts of Plato and Aristotle, who thought honey fell from the sky and was collected by bees. Winnie the Pooh was obsessed by it.

Use of man-made hives probably began in Egypt around 3,000 BC when people noticed swarms settling into holes in trees, and they offered alternative containers, hoping the bees would move in and therefore make it more convenient to rob them of honey. The practice quickly spread throughout the Old World where people offered baked clay cylinders or straw containers, and honeybees, who were drawn to dark, protected structures, moved right in. To get the honey from the cylinders, the beekeeper would smoke it to drive the bees out, enabling him to reach in with less chance of being stung. He'd rip the comb from the walls and smash it — eggs, larvae, pupae and queen — which meant the destruction of the next generation of the colony. When bees found their way into skeps — upside down baskets made of coiled straw or grass — they attached their comb directly to the inner walls, so extracting the honey meant squeezing the skep in a vise to wring out the honey. Any bees who hadn't been smoked out were squished most likely including the queen. The comb would be ruined and the colony would die.

Honey stealing evolved into *beekeeping* when it became obvious that it made more sense to find a way to extract honey but let the colony live and grow. The ancient Greeks were probably the first to use top bar moveable comb hives in which wooden bars were placed across the opening of a basket. The bees built comb suspended from each bar, keeping the queen and brood in the center combs as they would in the wild and stores of honey on the outer bars. A bar with honey-filled comb could be removed and crushed for the honey but leave the queen and brood intact.

In the quest for a "better" beehive — one capable of faster, more efficient honey production without destruction of any comb whatsoever — experimental box after experimental box using movable frames, was built during the 18th and 19th centuries. One recurring problem, however, was the not-so-little matter of how bees shore up their hive for warmth and protection from invaders. They plug small spaces with propolis and fill large spaces with burr comb — larger chunks of comb that glue the frames to the sides of the hive. A buildup of burr comb prevents a beekeeper from easily removing a frame.

It wasn't until the mid 19th century that a beehive was perfected which enabled the beekeeper not only to check his colony for disease, an aging queen, or imminent swarming, but to remove honey without destroying comb.

In the early part of that century, Francois Huber, a Swiss naturalist and blind observer of bees, brought a subtle but important observation to light, which the ancient Greeks apparently had known about. Fascinated by bees as a child, Huber maintained his interest even after going blind, and he continued his work with the help of a servant who became his eyes. Over many years he "observed" that honeybees kept free space between combs allowing easy maneuverability in order to clean the cells, feed the young and transport pollen and nectar. Huber ascertained that the interval separating the combs was a very specific measurement—just wide enough for bees to pass through, but not wide enough to make it necessary to fill with propolis.

Drawing on Huber's observation, the Rev. Lorenzo Langstroth in the mid-1800s labeled this concept "bee space" and proceeded to use the concept to perfect the movable frame hive. His design was a rectangular box with wooden frames suspended from the top of the box. By spacing the frames at the exact, correct bee space of 3/8" between the frames and on the top, bottom and sides of the box, the bees kept their precise corridors throughout, no longer needing to glue the frames together nor jam them with burr-comb to connect to the interior of the box. This provided the beekeeper easy removal of the frames without destroying any comb.

With that, commercial beekeeping took off like a drone chasing a queen. Hives were sturdy enough to be moved, supers could be added to increase room to make honey, frames could be put in a centrifugal extractor and then returned to the hive intact for the bees to refill. To add to the efficiency, wax foundation embossed with hexagons was placed on the frames to give the bees a jump-start on building comb.

Today, most beekeepers in the United States, both commercial and backyard, use Langstroth hives, whereas top bar hives, which are inexpensive and easy to build, are favored in developing countries. Recently, however, there has been a slight resurgence of interest in top bar hives among non-commercial beekeepers in the United States. Top bar hives may produce less honey, but some say they provide a more natural way to keep bees. Without the foundation used in Langstroth hives, bees build natural-sized cells, said to help in mite control. Comb hangs in the same U-shape as in the wild, and instead of sequestering the queen in one box, she has unbroken access to her whole colony.

In the past few years, as concern about the plight of the honeybee has reached the consciousness of many people in the Bay Area, the number of backyard and rooftop beekeepers who feel the desire to act individually has nearly tripled. Meet a few of these beekeepers — some who've been tending bees for decades, others who've come to it recently — as they generously share firsthand experiences in the complex, curious and fascinating world of the honeybee.

5
THE BEEKEEPERS

The higher the human intellect rises in the discovery [of the bees' aim], the more obvious it becomes that the final aim is beyond its reach.
                                        -Leo Tolstoy

THE BEEKEEPERS

The Rogue Beekeeper
David Eichorn, Kensington

I moved to Kensington in 1973 and a year later bought a hive out of *The Berkeley Barb* for $25. My mother had been a beekeeper, and I made bee equipment and helped her extract the honey when I was a kid. It must run in the family because my brother has fifteen hives in Big Sur. I have only two hives now. I've had up to twenty-five, but they were in out-yards, and recently I decided I only want to have bees in my own yard. From just those two hives I can get about 150 pounds of honey a year. I give it away to family and sell to neighbors and friends.

I've been called a "rogue" because beekeeping is illegal in this little square mile that's Kensington, but I do it anyway. Contra Costa County has an ordinance that makes beekeeping illegal, but cities can override this ordinance as most have done. Since Kensington is unincorporated, it's unable to change the ordinance, so it's subject to the laws of the county. I'm not worried about being found out. My neighbors know I have bees, and actually they're delighted because the bees pollinate their gardens and fruit trees.

> Bees and their lifestyle are mysterious, and anything mysterious is more interesting because there's always more to discover.

My honey, and the Bay Area's honey in general, is largely eucalyptus since there's so much of it, and it has a long, rich blooming season—December through June. Its nectar is high in sugar, and the honeybees love it. I have lots

33

of raspberries in my yard and citrus trees nearby, which they also love, so that gets mixed in. Environmentalists in the Bay Area are on a rip to get rid of the eucalyptus because it's an exotic tree, and they think it's taking over the old oaks and redwoods. Interestingly, eucalyptus doesn't need pollination, but bees love its nectar.

I've had a bee equipment business, and I've taught beekeeping for many years at Contra Costa College. I also teach private students in the spring. I have an observation hive which I take to classrooms and tell kids all about bees. They just love it, and I love to teach them. I'm also the go-to person in the East Bay to take unwanted swarms which, as a public service beekeeper, I find homes for.

People ask me why I'm a beekeeper. Beekeeping is endlessly fascinating, and I love it because it's a lifetime learning process. Bees and elephants are the two animals that just fascinate me. Bees and their lifestyle are mysterious, and anything mysterious is more interesting because there's always more to discover.

We all know there's an order in the hive—the queen's the queen, the workers do all the work. But there's just so much more. New bees that emerge from the larval stage immediately go to work in the hive doing cleanup. They clean the hive spotlessly, often needing to remove bees who have died in the hive. They're also responsible for making wax, building the comb and transferring nectar and pollen from the field bees.

Field bees fly back from their foraging with bellies full of nectar and pollen pockets full of pollen. The inside workers are right there at the entrance, some to take the nectar—mouth to mouth—others to take the pollen. And the field bees go right back out to get more. It's all perfectly timed and methodical. The house bees deposit the nectar and pack the pollen into cells to a certain depth, knowing to place it adjacent to the laying area of the queen so the bees who are feeding the larvae can easily get it. They mix it in a gland in their head and then exude the milky white substance—the exact right amount—into the cell for the worm to ingest; eventually it morphs into a larva. When you hold a frame to the light you see all the different shades of pollen—brown, yellow, orange, red, grey-blue—all mixed up in the cells. It's a beautiful multicolor array.

The house bees have eight wax glands and are the only ones capable of making wax because the field bees' wax glands atrophy. House bees ingest the nectar and make wax. When the nectar has evaporated to 80% sugar, all those cells that have the honey are capped with a very thin coat of beeswax which holds the honey in.

Honey is virtually indestructible in the atmosphere. It's been found in Egyptian pyramids that are thousands of years old. In fact, it may be the oldest food. Another mysterious thing...how do the bees know how to put just the right amount of acid into the honey to preserve it? It's been known for centuries that honey is antibacterial and can be applied to lesions and cuts.

Another group of house bees cap the larval cells with something that's not quite wax. It's a mixture—a brown color—that maybe has pitch in it. This is so the young bee can push through it when it's ready to emerge. It's fantastic to see it happen. Nobody helps it; the young bee struggles valiantly with its front legs and head to come out.

Drones have no jaw and no proboscis; they just sit around in the hive and are fed. It reminds me of bar flies — guys hanging around in bars begging drinks. For a long time I was resentful of drones; they give males a bad name, but they're actually the colony's insurance policy. If the queen is incapacitated for any reason—either injured or not competent to continue—a drone is needed to mate with a new queen, which the hive intuitively knows to generate. If she's not mated, she only makes drones and a hive cannot survive with only drones. She has to be mated to make females because it's the sperm that makes the females who are the workers. The queen has the magical ability to withhold sperm if she does want to lay drones, and the rest of the time she gives a little bit of that sperm to each egg to make a worker bee. At the height of the season, which is around May, the queen will lay 1,500-2,000 eggs a day. She just puts her rear end into a cell that's been cleaned and groomed and deposits an egg. Along comes a worker to feed royal jelly to the egg. It's precision timing.

The comb itself is mind-boggling. It's quite amazing that the bees can make these perfect hexagonal structures. The hexagonal cell is the absolute best shape. Inside the hexagon is the circle that holds the egg. If you think of the alternatives…a triangle can take a circle and is very strong, but there would be a lot of wasted space, and it would use a lot more wax. An octagon can take a circle, but octagons won't interlock and fit tightly together. A square could take a circle but would be too weak. The hexagon is absolutely perfect. It's the strongest, uses the least amount of wax and saves the greatest amount of space. It's the miracle shape. When I pick up a frame after I've taken the honey out it's the weight of a feather—so light and yet so strong and virtually indestructible. God, or whatever you want to say designed this, made the construction work perfectly.

When I go into the hive and pull out a frame of brood, I look at a laying pattern, and what I like to see is a complete plate with no cells that the queen has excluded. She's so well programmed that she lays an egg in every cell and doesn't hop around. Who knows whether she lays them by row or in a certain area at one time because you can't watch the queen. She won't lay an egg when you pull the frame out because she won't lay if there's light. Usually you're not lucky enough to see the queen at all.

Swarming is an amazing process. First of all, the Mother Queen slims down by laying lots of eggs so she'll be able to fly. She lays eggs in regular cells, but the workers, who have made two to five queen cells, move a fertilized egg that's less than 24 hours old into each of these cells. They're large, rough, vertically-hanging cells made out of the same material they use to cap the brood. To make the queen, they feed the egg more—at least that's what it appears—but we're not sure about that. Anyway, they feed them the right amount to create a queen. They have to keep the Mother Queen away from these cells so she won't sting them. The first virgin queen to emerge stings the sides of the other cells to kill them or, if by chance two emerge, they fight for dominance. A queen's stinger doesn't have barbs like the workers' stingers do, so it doesn't get stuck in what she stings, which would rip all the musculature out of her abdomen and pull her whole back end off, killing her.

When the new queen emerges and the hive feels confident that they're going to survive, the old Mother Queen takes off with one-third of the hive to find another place. This is the swarm. It's amazing to think of the timing of all this and how a third of the hive is "chosen" to leave.

I took a swarm the other day. When I take a swarm, the presumption is that the queen is in the swarm, so I act as if she's in there. I went to look the next day and there on the lid was the queen. I didn't know why she was there—she belonged inside the hive—but there she was, and she was quite small and black. I was very nervous. As a beekeeper I'm very cautious when working around the queen. You don't want to damage her in any way because a swarm, which doesn't have a hive yet, has no way of generating another queen, so they're particularly vulnerable at that point. I saw this beautiful little black queen walk down into the hive, and I wasn't anxious anymore.

I haven't seen a black queen in quite a while. It's unusual, although it's merely a minor genetic difference. It doesn't seem to make a difference in honey production, inclination to swarm, early spring buildup or disease resistance. It's just a variation in coloring. I favor them because they're rare. It means half the genetic makeup of the bees she's producing is black, but we don't know what the male composition of her eggs is. She gets mated up to five times, so some of her offspring might be all black, but probably mostly a mixture.

All this behavior is genetically programmed. A bee's brain is the size of a pinhead. There's very little, if any, learned behavior, but bees are very adaptive. They have reactive ability, but apparently don't think. I certainly like to think something did the original programming.

I could go on forever.... This is why I'm a beekeeper.

THE BEEKEEPERS

Perfumer & Beekeeper
Laurie Stern, El Cerrito

Ever since honeybees came to our garden several years ago, it's been so much fuller and richer. In fact, they've made my garden absolutely thrive. Bees can forage for miles, and I'm sure these bees go elsewhere in addition to all they find here, but they always come back to the hive in our garden. It's their home.

I originally saw them as a swarm right in the middle of the tomato patch. I didn't know what a swarm was; I just saw this big wad of bees. I wasn't afraid of them, but they stayed and stayed, and I realized I'd better deal with it. Being the total nature lover that I am, I certainly wouldn't poison them, although I know a lot of people do. Then I found David Eichorn on the Internet, and called him to take them away.

> I've heard from other beekeepers that the feel of bees on you is wonderful. If bees feel safe with you, the feel of them on your hands is like the softest, lightest, sweetest kind of touch. Someday I'd like to feel that.

When he came to remove them he started telling me about them—"these are foraging bees, these are fanning the hive...." I found it so fascinating that by the time he was ready to take them away I knew I wanted them to stay. He also mentioned they tend to swarm to a place that's an ideal environment for them, so I thought I should make them a home here. He tried to discourage me because keeping bees can be a fair amount of work; you have to pay attention and be aware of what's going on. He finally agreed to teach me, and I hired him on retainer. He and I built my hive in his workshop so I could learn every aspect of beekeeping. I started with that hive and then got another.

I've always loved flowers and gardens. My husband and I have these extensive gardens that go down the slope of the hill and are filled with many different flowers. I had a wedding flower business for years but ended it ten years ago. Now I have a botanical perfume business named Velvet and Sweet Pea's Purrfumery, which is named after two of our cats. I make perfumes from essential oils and floral tinctures from our garden, so to have this bee swarm come to me felt magical and somehow auspicious.

One summer when my parents were visiting, the bees were on the lavender near the entrance to the guesthouse, and my dad was worried about my mom getting stung. I told him, if you don't hurt them they won't hurt you, and my father said, "I can't believe it; you said the exact same thing when we were showing you tigers in the zoo years ago." That's my philosophy, and I think that's why the bees came here.

My beloved bees disappeared after living here for four years. We couldn't find any residue of any kind of disease; both hives just disappeared. I knew one of them wasn't doing very well, but the other one was really strong. I had been checking them every couple of days and thought everything was fine. It was sad, I have to say, and I was pretty devastated, which I know sounds crazy. I took it quite personally, actually; I felt abandoned. They had come to me so personally, and their leaving also felt personal, but I realize bees are really just like a wild animal; we have no control over them. We don't understand their hardwiring or what makes them stay or go.

After they disappeared, I did the extraction from the hives because there was a lot of honey and wax. Here was this gorgeous honey, and I was wondering what I might have done to make them disappear.

At that time in my life I was incredibly busy between my perfume making, my cat rescue, family, relatives, my husband, everything. I was overwhelmed and thought maybe I should take a break from having bees for a year or so. But I missed them so much and realized when I went into the garden, without them there, it was as if I didn't have a destination. The garden, even though it was full of life, felt as if it had lost its soul.

Seeing how devastated I was, Gary offered to take over the beekeeping if we got more hives. I knew I'd have to help since I've been doing it longer and know more, but I was thrilled, especially if he could take over the extraction, which is a very long, intensive day.

He could also handle the swarms, which always happen at the worst time imaginable like when you're having twenty people over for brunch and suddenly you notice 50,000 bees swarming into the air. As a conscientious beekeeper you're responsible for your swarms and you have to jump to it immediately. It's like running after a wayward child with everyone watching. Once I was having a birthday breakfast for a friend for her sixtieth birthday with ten people coming. I was getting everything ready, and suddenly the bees swarmed into my neighbor's yard. She happens to be allergic to bees. "Okay, Gary," I said, "take over on the brunch. I've got to go deal with the swarm."

This spring, my friend Pat's bees were swarming like mad. Her hives had started from my swarms from the bees who left. I had caught one of them last year, hived it, and brought it to her. When she started having swarms, she gave me a wonderful one. Then that hive swarmed, which they don't usually do that fast because a swarm doesn't usually swarm. We gave that one to Pat. Our exchange of related swarms was kind of incestuous, if you ask me.

At that point, I was thinking we'll have just one hive, but then I decided that we should actually have two, because if one of them isn't strong, you can take brood frame from the stronger hive and put it in the weaker. So I got another swarm from Pat, which was really tiny but I thought I'd try it. Unfortunately, that one didn't do very well. One day Gary went down to check on them and saw there were robber bees going into the hive as the other bees were coming out. They were literally fighting and killing each other. It was just horrible to watch. I saw all the little dead bodies on the ground. My friend, who calls me the "Jewish Mother of Beekeeping," asked me if I had buried each one and given them a ceremony. Thankfully, we caught the situation immediately, put hive reducers on and the robber bees left. A hive reducer is a small piece of wood that makes the entrance to the hive a lot smaller and only allows a couple of bees to go in, so the resident bees have lot more ability to fight robbers off. Usually you put it on in the winter, because if it gets very cold or rainy, the hive stays warmer.

The robber bees left, but the hive didn't make it. David told me it had foulbrood. The part with the foulbrood was all semi-capped cells, but there was nothing in them. They were very dark brown with a little hole in each.

David found us another swarm; this one was really large. They're doing fantastic, building a new frame and brood. Now both hives are strong, and I'm very happy because Gary's taking over more and more.

Gary is an incredible, natural beekeeper. I suit up completely when I go into the hives because I don't want to be nervous, but Gary is kind of macho and says he doesn't need a suit. It turns out he's right. He's the quintessential beekeeper, and without wearing a suit, veil or gloves he's able to bring the frames out really slowly and carefully. I was really careful, too, but Gary's even slower than I was, and very delicate, concentrated, careful, and very connected with the bees. A lot of the best beekeepers don't wear suits and veils because they're so gentle. I've heard that the feel of bees on you is wonderful. If bees feel safe and not threatened, the feel of them on your hands is like the softest, lightest, sweetest kind of touch. Some day I'd like to feel that.

The bees make the most exquisite honey. My husband and I are complete honey addicts so it's a good thing we have bees. Every morning for breakfast we eat Greek yogurt drizzled with honey and fruit from our fruit trees. At this point we're beyond addicted, but at least it's one of the healthiest foods on the planet. Gary jokes that our honey would be $100 a jar at the rate we produce.

Only when you threaten them or do something really idiotic do honeybees sting. For example, if I were to go into the hive in the winter to get some honey, they'd be rightfully threatened. They don't have an abundance of honey then and need to protect their food supply. Other than that, they're really friendly. Their flight path is through where we walk but it's never a problem. We have a relationship.

We have several fountains and birdbaths for them because they need water. I have corks floating around so they have little boats to land on. If they don't feel like floating they just stand on the edge and drink.

I've heard that a garden flourishes if you have both wild bees and honeybees. Wild bees, which include bumblebees, pollinate so many flowers and herbs. In conjunction with honeybees it's ideal because there's so much pollination going on, and that strengthens the plants. I just love the bumblebees—how they get pollen all over their velvety bodies. I read somewhere that if you have an old teapot that breaks and you bury it with the spout sticking out of the ground, the wild bees will find it, and it'll make a nice, dark home for them. I love that idea. Someday I'm going to have an area with all the little teapot spouts sticking up.

The other amazing substance honeybees make is propolis or bee-glue, which they produce by adding sap and resin they've gathered from trees to a little honey, and it turns into this goopy stuff. They use it to plug any holes in the hive. It seals the hive from predators and ants and helps it stay a steady temperature. David used to sell it to someone who repaired Stradivarius violins because it's such an amazing sealant.

I scrape dried, crusty propolis off the edges of the hive and make some of my perfumes with it. I grind it all up and put it in organic grape alcohol, let it sit for about six months, strain it and use it as a tincture in my perfumes. I have a honey perfume, and the propolis slows down the evaporation. I use beeswax for my solid perfumes. I mix essential oils into jojoba oil, heat it, grate in beeswax, and it makes it solid like an unguent. Whenever I'm making my natural perfumes, I feel like a bee buzzing flower to flower combining all of these aromatic treasures from the garden together and distilling them into one delicious nectar.

When people think of beekeepers they think of commercial operations, not what we're doing here in our back yards. We're definitely not doing it for the money! It would be great if more people kept bees on a backyard scale because it would help the bees, flowers, fruits, herbs, and vegetables so much. It's hard work, but I find it satisfying in so many ways—communication with a wild, magical creature, the wonderful honey and the tremendous help it gives to the environment. It's also endlessly interesting; you never stop learning. The more I learn, the more I realize there is to learn! It's amazing and astounding—every part of it. Bees are still completely wild; we think we manage them, but there's still such a wildness to them that I respect and love that about them. Cats have that too. There's nature in there that just won't be tamed. Most importantly, I would like people to appreciate and respect honeybees more and fear them less. They only sting when threatened and really just want to go about their business of pollinating and making honey to feed their young.

It's amazing—it rains into the ground, the plant draws in the moisture, the moisture comes up through the flower filled with minerals, vitamins and essential oils, and it becomes this beautiful nectar. The bees sip it, bring it back to the hive and make it into honey by drawing the moisture out of it. The plants need to attract the bees in order to survive, and the bees need the nectar and pollen to survive. In turn, we need bees to survive. We're all so interdependent and interconnected.

People say honeybees are hardwired, genetically programmed. To me that isn't enough of an explanation for their amazing behavior; it misses the mystery. How bees figure things out is incredible; for example, when they're searching for a new home, the scout bees go out to look and when they come back they do a dance to tell the other bees how far away this ideal place is. Several bees come back with a report on different places, and then they communally decide which place to go. If this is all genetically programmed how can a group decision be programmed? If the bee isn't thinking, somebody originally did. I don't know what I believe about God...it's a mystery, and I'm fine with that, but when I see what the bees do, I think there's some magical force, an original design. The whole natural world blows me away constantly. There's a method to it; every animal and plant has some kind of gift or signature that makes it unique.

All I really know for sure is my garden is my sanctuary and my little paradise. It's pretty heavenly out here and sometimes I wonder why I ever leave. I love all of these wild little creatures in my life! I'm very thankful to the honeybees for making life so much more delicious!

Floral Designer & Beekeeper
Patricia Gibbons, El Cerrito

It was in the early spring of 2007 that my husband Mike and I began to notice an unusual amount of bee activity in our back yard. We watched more closely and saw that bees were coming in and out of a plaster of paris container that we were using as a plant stand. The bees found a small opening (and that's all it takes) which gave them access to the round, dark, empty interior—a perfect place for building a small hive. I had some reservations about keeping bees and what that would involve because I was afraid of getting stung but quickly got used to them being a part of our lives. As Mike said, "It's as if they adopted us, saying 'oh, this is a good place to hang out, let's live here.'" And that was the beginning!

We had already spoken to our neighbors about keeping bees and no one minded that 40,000 new creatures had taken up residence in our yard.

This certainly wasn't your typical modern hive; it was similar to the conical shaped beehives the ancient Greeks and Egyptians used to weave from straw and grass. The container was 12" high with a 12" diameter, open at each end, tube-like. We placed a board over the top to protect the bees from the elements. Viewed from above, the honeycomb didn't have any pattern but when flipped over, you could see the remarkably organized combs hanging vertically down from the "roof" of the container. With such a small hive we weren't able to harvest honey without disturbing them.

Because it was so small, it soon became over-crowded and led to swarming. The first time the bees swarmed I was hanging laundry. Suddenly I heard a loud buzzing sound. I looked up to see a large, dense moving mass of bees slowly rising up into the air. It was an amazing sight and sound, and at that time, not knowing anything about bees, I put the laundry basket over my head and ran into the house. Later I learned that swarming bees are gorged with honey, making it almost impossible to sting and that I was quite safe. They landed in a neighbor's pine tree, temporarily, until they moved on once again to parts unknown.

We tried to get the remaining bees to move into a standard hive, which would give them more space. We cut a hole in the bottom board of the top hive and placed it over the existing hive to encourage the bees to move upwards, which is their natural tendency. They refused to move in, obviously preferring the small, warm space they created. These bees were very gentle, and I was quite comfortable being close to them without any fear of being stung. Eventually and sadly, the bees didn't make it through the winter, but by then Mike and I were both hooked and decided to become beekeepers.

The following spring, we decided to start again. We got a swarm from our friend and fellow beekeeper, Laurie, and set up a standard hive. Eventually this hive also swarmed, and we didn't get any honey the second year. While there is a debate whether swarming is a good thing or not, we've gotten quite good at capturing them (with help from friends), and there is always someone who needs more bees. Most of the swarms landed in our yard or in a neighbor's yard. We had already spoken to our neighbors about keeping bees, and no one minded that 40,000 new creatures had taken up residence in our yard. They all seem to enjoy their presence, which has the added bonus of having their fruit trees and gardens flourish.

Once a swarm landed in a jasmine bush, and they were quite difficult to remove. Laurie came over to help, and we tried "scooping" up bees, hoping the queen was among them. We dropped the bees into a small carrying case called a nuc box, which is used to collect and transport swarms. When bees swarm, they cluster around the queen, protecting her, and wherever the queen is, that's where the rest of the bees will follow. We ended up building a ramp from the vines, where most of the bees were still gathered, to the nuc box. It took a couple of days, but they eventually all made it into the box. It's thought that these particular bees may have swarming in their genes because even when there's plenty of room in the hives, they're making queen cells and swarming. Laurie and I have been passing bees to each other all season.

By the summer of 2010 after taking bee classes and reading many books, we had our first honey harvest from our three hives: seven frames, which was close to 25 pounds of honey, which we shared with neighbors and friends and still had plenty for us.

I've come to love having the bees and enjoy watching them collect nectar and pollen. A great time to watch them is in early afternoon, when the young bees take their "maiden flight." They start out by flying in small circles, gradually building up distance from the hive as they learn to identify their surroundings.

Gradually, I've been transitioning my garden to bring in more bee-friendly plants. We're lucky in the Bay Area because there is an abundance of flowers that grow well and provide ample nectar and pollen. The bees especially love a nearby eucalyptus grove, which flowers over the winter and provides a needed source of food during that time. It's been a new focus for me—I had my first garden when I was five, filling my red wagon with violets, johnny jump-ups, wild asparagus and strawberries. I still have some of the same types of plants in my garden now—fond remembrances of that early start. There are many fruit and citrus trees in the neighborhood, as well as redbud — all favorites of bees. Our back yard has an established garden which includes a large mock orange tree, hardenbergia, germander, catmint and mallow which are covered with bees in the spring. There's also California lilac, thyme, lamb's ear, lavender, rosemary and oregano which are a few of their other favorites.

What the bees are foraging affects the flavor of the honey, and all the local honey I've tried has a slightly different taste. Eucalyptus gives a light, sweet taste — quite delicious! It's been found that bees are attracted to gardens that have a variety of around ten of their favorite plants, grown in patches with successive blooming seasons. Every spring there's a Bay Area native garden tour where one can visit gardens which showcase native plants.

Since learning about bees, I've also discovered that a large percentage of native California bees live in the ground. I've removed mulch from certain areas in my garden because the bees require undisturbed, bare earth in order to build their tunnels and live. There are around 25,000 bee species in the world, with around 1,500 in California, of which approximately 80 are native. Bee gardens are getting more popular, and one can create a beautiful setting for oneself while providing food for bees.

The Beekeeping Gene
Steve Gentry, Orinda

I've always been oriented around critters, so it's no wonder I fell in love with honeybees. I was the kind of kid who went fishing at the lake after school and walked home with a frog in his pocket. That was old Orinda, back in the fifties, in the days when kids could walk home alone.

I remember going on a Boy Scout excursion to the Natural Science building at Lake Merritt when I was twelve. It was there I saw the observation beehive, which made quite an impression on me and got me interested in keeping bees. You walked up two steps and looked inside. I was just amazed at all the activity and the shape of the comb. I remember thinking, *if I ever get a chance to do this, I will, because I want to know everything about bees.*

> It's a passion...every day there's some kid who comes by and you can't unglue him from the face of the observation hive. It's like their feet are lead and they're not going anywhere.

When I was around thirty, I bought my first house in Pleasant Hill and took a short course on honeybees and what was going on inside a beehive. There were ten of us in the course, and after it was over, we put our names on a list so we could keep track of each other and buy equipment cheaper if we bought in bulk. That group eventually became the Mt. Diablo Beekeepers Association. Today we have 240 members and I think we're the biggest bee club west of the Rockies. I'm the only founding member who's still there, which I'm proud of. Half have died and others just drifted off.

I got my first bees that spring after the course. A couple of years later, I wanted to build an observation hive that I could take to classrooms—a walk-around box with a frame of bees and a marked queen. We had some old timers in our club, so I phoned some of them because I knew they had all the old knowledge. One was Virgil Philipi who worked in El Sobrante, and I asked him if he knew anything about building an observation beehive. He said, "Yeah, I know a little about building an observation hive; I built one down at Lake Merritt in 1945 when I got back from the war." I had known Virgil for two years, but I didn't know he had built the hive that I had been so spellbound with twenty years earlier as a Boy Scout. I thought it was great that the energy had gone around and come back.

    I always bring an observation beehive to the farmers' markets where I sell my honey. I've been keeping bees for a long time—thirty years—and twenty of those years I've been carrying bees around in this hive. The love of bees is mysterious. Some people look at them and get scared; other people are indifferent, and then there are those who are enthralled with them. I've noticed that one out of a hundred kids is mesmerized. It's a passion, and not everybody has a passion for any particular thing, but every day there's some kid who comes by and you can't unglue him from the face of the observation hive. It's like their feet are lead and they're not going anywhere. Some of them are as young as three years old; some as old as fifteen. The joy for me is imagining that I'm the kid standing in front of my observation beehive and looking inside, getting the thrill I remember as a twelve-year-old. I hope all these kids become beekeepers, and I like to think I had something to do with it, just like Virgil. It's a nice energy to pass on.

    What's good about bees is everybody's got an opinion. So whether it's positive or negative, if you're a teacher—and I consider myself a teacher—if it's a negative energy, you can make hay out of that. If it's a positive energy, you can make hay quicker out of it. It's the energy behind it that's important, not the attitude, because you can change the attitude, but you can't change the passion. That's the fun part of it, to see that passion in a kid's eyes.

When kids are afraid of bees because they think they might get stung, you educate them. You educate their eyeballs. You tell them what they're looking at. If they're looking at a busy hive where the bees are clearly not interested in stinging anybody, they'll catch on. I have a bunch of lectures that I give. In years past, it has gone from the Zen of beekeeping to the bee whisperer, because people understand that jargon. Spreading the love of bees is my passion.

***

Honey is a very, very clean food. It's good stuff. Bees are extremely hygienic and there's nothing cleaner than the inside of a beehive. I not only harvest honey, but I also capture pollen, which most beekeepers don't do because it's time consuming. Pollen is an amazing substance. If you're a runner, it's an enormous stimulant. In food, it's pure protein with all these little micro-vitamins. Through collecting pollen I've been able to see that bees can learn.

When I put my pollen traps on, there's a screen that bees go through, which is too small for them to fit unless they drop their pollen pockets, and that's how you get pollen. The first day you put the pollen trap on, they have to drop a hundred percent of their pollen, because otherwise they can't get through the trap. But the bees that are bringing pollen in have a job to do, and they're very serious about it. So within hours, certainly within the next day, half of the bees bringing pollen back have learned they can get in if they don't bring a full load. So they bring part of a load. By the third day, all of the bees that are foragers bringing pollen back for the brood are carrying half loads. I'm not getting any pollen, but at least some of the pollen is getting into the hive, which, of course, is what I want.

So then you have to open the trap. The day you open the trap, they're still bringing in half loads. The next day, some of the bees are still bringing half loads, and by the third day, they're all bringing full loads again.

So then you close the trap. The trap is open for three days and closed for three days, then open for three days and closed for three days. That's the way you run a pollen trap.

I've been recommending local honey for nose allergies for years. It's an old, old, old remedy, and now even Kaiser doctors are recommending it. My theory is that it's probably partly a mild immune booster and partly a desensitizer too. Probably a quarter to a third of the people that I sell honey to are buying it as a remedy. They like the honey, but they are buying it because it helps them get over their nose allergies by taking a teaspoon a day. It seems that good honey that hasn't been roasted and overly filtered is a mild immune booster, and it's your immune system that's deficient when you have nose allergies.

My primary intention in harvesting honey is not making money; partly I do it because it's "old time religion." I like talking about old things, I guess. I like tradition. I don't really make that much money at the farmers' markets but my presence there does put a face on my label at Whole Foods. I get a double benefit there because it's just a fun thing to do. It gives me access to a lot of people, and I like yakking about bees.

I specifically try to make different varietal honeys. It's less efficient, but I want to make chamise honey or madrone honey or star thistle honey or any of these honeys that you don't normally see on the shelf like clover, citrus, sage, alfalfa or buckwheat. Those are all commercial honeys. I call them commercial because if you're in the pollination business, which is where the money is (it's certainly not in honey production) and you've got three thousand hives, it's actually cheaper to haul those hives up to Montana and have the bees gorge on clover, make more bees and then bring them back to do pollination. The same thing with sage out in Nevada or buckwheat down between L.A. and San Diego, or alfalfa and clover in big grazing crops.

So those are all crops that the big business beekeeper will find, and it's free food for the bees. All you do is get the bees there, and they'll feed on that food. It's cheaper than mixing up sugar water to feed them. It's just a matter of economics. They sell the excess, and that's what you see on the shelf.

Commercial beekeepers' attitude towards honey is very compromised. There are not too many other crops that are big enough to feed that many bees. So you don't see the really, really nice honeys that you would have seen a hundred years ago when they didn't move bees around. The local beekeeper would be like the local butcher. Whatever honey came out of his hives in that town was the honey you got. He wasn't out there looking for anything else.

It wasn't until World War I that General Motors made big trucks. After the war the United States started making roads big enough to handle the volume of traffic and the weight of the trucks that would travel on them. Suddenly the farmers got bigger, the field crops got bigger and the orchards got bigger. They got more efficient because they had bigger trucks to haul things. So the forty-acre farms from the 1840s became four hundred acres in 1910. They finally became four thousand acres and forty thousand acres. They just got bigger and bigger.

Beekeeping followed right along. They got trucks; they could put bees on the trucks and move them. The migratory beekeepers would move from Florida clear up into Saskatchewan, which was the last crop. When it got cold, they'd move all hives back to Florida and start the whole thing again in the spring next year. Of course, these were the bee colonies that were collapsing.

I have anywhere between a hundred and a hundred and fifty hives in people's back yards. There are a lot of people who come to me and are sold on the idea of having bees in their backyards. They don't necessarily want to be beekeepers, but they do like the idea of having bees. I have certain parameters, like whether I can get a pick-up truck in there. It has to be at least a pick-up load of bees, which is ten hives.

If I can, I'll move bees to a place that has a special crop. If I find a place that is right next to a huge eucalyptus grove and I know when that grove goes off, well, I'll move ten hives over there just to pick up eucalyptus honey. If it seems not too many other things are in bloom, then I can label it "eucalyptus honey." If there are too many other plants with their nectar flow still on, I just call it "wildflower".

Of course, it's not a hundred percent. But if it's over fifty percent I tell people that it's fifty percent eucalyptus. I can guesstimate it, but it doesn't really matter; it certainly has a distinct flavor. Other fifty percent flavors that I might have are star thistle, madrone, chamise, which are from undeveloped wildlands.

But then down in areas like in San Ramon, in Bollinger Canyon, there are big housing tracts. The bees can fly up into the park where they forage for star thistle especially in the summer, but they can also fly downhill to the backyards where people irrigate. So you get backyard honey. There's an old guy in Lafayette that coined the term "suburban floral mix" which means anything that's blooming in your backyard. I thought that was a cute term.

***

My father told me my grandfather was an early Mormon in a little town named Beaver in southern Utah. My father was born in 1900, and apparently my grandfather and grandmother went their separate ways leaving him to be raised by his brothers. Consequently, there weren't a lot of stories passed down, and he never knew much about his own family. He did know, however, that his father brought my great-grandfather, who was an early pioneer mechanic and blacksmith, to a little town named Minersville.

Minersville is about twenty miles off the beaten track. I had never been there, and when I was driving around the West about four years ago I thought I'd stop in this town and see what I could find about my great-grandfather and grandmother who was raised there.

I asked around for information about this town and found out that there was a book written in the fifties about the families that came in, how they got started, and what they did. I found a two-page chapter on pioneer beekeeping in the 1850-1870 era in Minersville, Utah, and in the first paragraph was my grandmother's name, and in the next paragraph was her father, my great-grandfather.

It was incredible. I almost dropped the book. I still can't believe it. It turns out my father didn't know that his mother and her father were pioneer beekeepers in southern Utah at the turn of the century. My father was an attorney, and he was completely unconscious when it came to insects; everything was something to be squished. It's unbelievable, very bizarre. What are the odds of having that pop up three times in four generations or twice in two generations? It might lead one to think there's a beekeeping gene!

***

Every two years, there's a world meeting of beekeepers, called Apimondia. Seven years ago, the meeting was in Lubiana, Slovania, and I decided to go. Several years before, at the Orinda Farmers' Market, I had met a French beekeeper and his wife who came here every other year to visit friends, so over the years I got to know them. He invited me to come visit him on my way back from Apimondia. I flew into Paris, took the train across to Slovania, and on my way back I visited him at his home north of Provence. He's a chef and has ten hives. I spent two weeks at his home, a primitive stone house from the sixteenth century. It was a wonderful experience.

Apimondia changes locations. Last September it was in Montpelier in the south of France, and I went. The French beekeeper had moved to a warmer climate down on the Mediterranean, about a twenty-minute drive from Montpelier so again I spent two weeks at his house.

There were ten thousand beekeepers from all over the world at Apimondia because everybody wanted to go to the south of France. People from Taiwan, Japan, China, South America, Africa, Canada, the United States and all over Europe came. It was unbelievable. The whole town was converted to beekeeping. When you get that many people together, with all these scientific papers about beekeeping being given, beekeeping wares sold, and everybody yakking about the same thing for seven days, it's an experience you won't forget. A lot of bee energy. We were like one big hive with one shared purpose!

The Philosopher Beekeeper
Eli Waddle, San Francisco

I'm a landscape gardener and one of the gardens I tend is in Pacific Heights. About two weeks before the honeybees arrived at my house I realized I hadn't seen any in this garden for a long time. Usually I see them all over flowering cherries, plums and lavender. I had seen wild bees, but not honeybees, and I was thinking maybe Colony Collapse had gotten to the West Coast. One day I saw three honeybees gathering pollen inside a patch of white poppies. I started talking to them (gardeners often do this!) and told them I was so happy to see them, that I had been worried and that it was good to know there was a hive around here somewhere. I told them I had just planted a vegetable garden and suggested they tell their friends to come over and pollinate it. I watched a little longer until they flew away. A week later they accepted my invitation and moved into my house.

> In just three weeks, they had built seven combs hanging from the ceiling and dropping about six feet. Comb is very different when it's not on a frame. It looks like a lung or a heart—definitely some kind of organ you'd find inside a body.

I was sitting at my desk looking out at the vegetable garden when I heard what sounded like a thousand weed wackers. I assumed it was the handyman, but it seemed so excessive that I went out to see what was happening. The entire front yard looked like it was snowing bees. I hurried back inside, shut all the windows but could still hear the buzz of thousands and thousands of bees.

I watched, totally mesmerized, until gradually there was some movement towards the side of the house. When the noised lessened, I went out and saw an amazing sight— alongside the building was a solid swath of bees about two feet wide, ten feet tall and two feet deep. They had all landed on the house and one by one were climbing into an opening in a knot hole. It took over an hour for every single bee to get into the wall. If I hadn't been there in that hour I probably never would have know there were 20,000 bees in my wall since they fly out only a few bees at a time.

I certainly didn't want them exterminated but also didn't particularly want thousands of bees nesting in my house. It's an old building, and there were probably lots of ways to get through the sheetrock into my rooms. When I told my landlord about them he was really excited and suggested cutting a piece of wall out and fitting it with plexiglass so we could watch them. I knew he was hooked and wouldn't exterminate them either, but I felt it was better that they go live in a hive, not in the house, so I called a beekeeper who was expert at removing swarms. He explained why they had picked that particular spot. Bees like to get an early start in the morning, and that wall faces east so the sun would hit early. Also, they like to be up high for protection against predators. He said that since they had just made a stressful journey to their new home, they should have several weeks to build honeycomb and rest from swarming before he moved them into their new hives. He'd return in three weeks.

Meanwhile, I got some equipment and learned as much as I could about honeybees. I live in a unique situation that's perfect for keeping bees. I rent from former landscaping clients who have several buildings with extensive grounds up in the hills overlooking the valley.

Three weeks later Philip came back, fully regaled in bee suit, gloves and veil. He had concocted a custom made vacuum made out of a half horse power shop vac so it was low enough suction that it wouldn't hurt the bees. He had built a little wooden box with screens on three sides and a sliding wooden bottom to vacuum them into. As neighbors and friends gathered round, he gently cut the dry wall from the inside of my study. Everyone held their breath, poised to run as we gasped at the sight of thousands of bees. All motion stopped for a second as the bees hovered...and then went right back to work, obviously sensing no threat. The removal was done in the day while many of the bees were out working. I wondered what would happen at night when they came back and found the hole plugged up, but Philip assured me they'd find their new hive. Bees are experts at communicating with each other and would figure it out.

Once they were all safely vacuumed into the box we saw the comb. It was absolutely astounding. In just three weeks, they had built seven combs, hanging from the ceiling and dropping about six feet. Comb is very different when it's not on a frame. It looks like a lung or a heart — definitely some kind of organ you'd find inside a body. The wax is very white when they first make it and very beautiful. Philip nearly had a heart attack when he saw they had attached some comb to an electric wire.

The combs were full of eggs, larvae and honey. There were new bees ready to hatch, just beginning to chew through the wax. Philip cut the comb carefully out of wall and saved it in large chunks which we pressed on empty frames and held them in using rubber bands. Basically we just gave the bees their old home back in a new box. The box of bees weighed about five pounds and one good shake over the new hive and the bees were all in. They sounded like a pile of dried leaves as they all dropped in. At first they were slightly agitated, but once they realized nothing was threatening them, recognized their own honeycomb and knew their queen was there, they just went down into the frames and carried on as if nothing had happened.

I bought a second swarm, but it didn't do very well. It's best to have two colonies so if one is stronger and the other needs help, you just lift a comb out of the stronger and put in the weaker as long as you brush off any bees. Bees don't seem to mind each others' larvae or honey, but they'll fight to the death if bees from a separate colony are introduced. The inserted frame will give the weaker hive more bees once the larvae hatch.

From the first hive, which was incredibly strong, I've gotten several swarms. Now I have five hives which is definitely enough for now. My family is growing too fast.

I'm a very spiritual person. Because I spent my childhood out in nature all the time, and because of the work I do, I feel really connected to the natural environment, and, like other living things, can sense when someone's interested in them. I know as far as gardens go, when the garden is loved —it's as basic as that—and there's a connection with the humans around it, the plants perform better. Animals and people are certainly the same way—they do better when they're not neglected.

It makes me sad every time I accidentally squish a bee or cause it to sting me and therefore die—a tiny life extinguished. There's suffering and pain, but I prefer not to cause it. I feel a very strong presence when a bee flies into my house or buzzes around me. Whether that's me anthropomorphizing the bee or actually feeling its soul, I don't know. I try not to be arrogant about other creatures and always assume they have their own destiny and life to lead, so I respect them and make way for them.

Everything has some kind of soul. I believe everything is connected and made out of the same stuff and keeps working its way through the universe in different forms. It's possible to recognize these common elements in other beings and to feel connected in that way. I think our physical life is a metaphor for something larger. Bees seem to act as a group with one mind, one purpose and many bodies to carry out that purpose. The same could be said of humans if we looked at ourselves from a distance.

The more I learn about bees the more I'm bewildered by how scientists and behavioral experts believe humans are the most intelligent force in the universe. It's amazing what these insects, who live for only two months, can accomplish. They already know what to do when they're born. It's generally called programming, but I call it intelligence because I believe there are many different kinds of intelligence that most people refuse to accept. We're very arrogant. I suppose the more time I spend with bees and plants, the more I'm amazed this world exists at all. We're really lucky to be here, and we need to stop destroying the planet because we're not going to get another chance.

The Patient Beekeeper
Leah Fortin, Oakland

I want to do anything I can do to make the world a more beautiful place. I keep bees because I'm a gardener, and I absolutely adore flowers, which certainly make things more beautiful. The bees keep my flowers growing, and I've also become very fond of the bees.

I had read an article about almond growers in California just before almond season began in February. It was about how growers needed to rent bee boxes because all of a sudden they needed hundreds of thousands of bees to pollinate the almond groves. They were getting the hives from a variety of sources, and I thought what a fun way that could be to make some money. At the time I was working as a consultant and wasn't very happy with my job, so I entertained the idea. I look back now and think it was a crazy idea, but I wasn't the only person who thought of it.

> I never hide that I'm a beekeeper; I want people to know and would rather have a confrontation with someone about bees so I can show them how safe and important they are to nature.

I went to an Alameda County Beekeeping Association meeting where I talked to a bee broker. Bee brokers help coordinate the shipment of bees to the almond growers. She said people were shipping out boxes from Florida, Texas, Michigan and other states, and they'd arrive completely busted apart. She wasn't sure they even had contracts with the almond growers.

The almond growers needed hundreds and hundreds of boxes. Because they're mono-crop growers, they suddenly have to bring honeybees in from all over. If I were an almond grower and knew I needed bees for my crop in February and March, then in April I'd grow something else for the bees to sustain them the rest of the year and keep them around until the next almond season. But almond growers have such a corporate mentality that they have to rent hives; they'll pay up to $150 per box. That's what first got me interested, but I soon discovered I was certainly not interested in doing volume and renting hives out to mono-crop growers.

When I first started keeping bees I realized how much I loved it despite the fact that I learned about beekeeping by trial and error—mostly error. At first, I lost more hives than I was able to keep; in fact, I lost two hives the first year I had them. One hive just flew off, and I have no idea why.

My other hive was on my roof because I have such a teeny yard. The bees seemed so happy; they stuck around for a really long time. My family and I were fascinated by them, so we were lifting the lid and looking in the hive all the time. They're just always so busy and purposeful. I'd go up a lot and peek in to see them work the hive, and my daughter would go up there to show her friends. The bees probably sensed the light and the changing of their habitat too frequently. They like to be snug and cozy, so I'm sure they got annoyed by so much opening of the box, didn't appreciate it, and flew off. After they were gone I still had lots of healthy bees in my garden, and I could see the same patterns of what my rooftop bees had been eating, so I suspect they were returning to my garden.

My third hive had mites, but a fellow beekeeper taught me how to treat them. We used powdered sugar sprinkled into the boxes and the bees, who like to keep things nice and clean, eat the sugar and the mites drop off as the bees pluck at the sugar. The mites aren't so much a problem in the bee box, but if they go into the comb where the larvae are, they take up space, and the wings of the developing larvae become deformed so they can't fly.

THE BEEKEEPERS

Once you start keeping bees you meet all these other beekeepers. A neighbor around the corner keeps bees, and my friend Peter who lives two blocks down keeps several hives, plus we have a box together. Peter and I share different hives around town. We get our bees naturally from swarms, so we know we're getting bees that are ultimately healthy rather than ones that are "harvested." You can buy a queen or even a hive from commercial outfits, but when you get a natural swarm—one that's flown off from another local hive because they've created a second queen—you've got a natural, healthy hive that's native to Oakland. They're used to what they've been eating, so they'll stay here.

Several years ago I got a swarm and put it in a box at Marsha Donahue's garden in Berkeley. Marsha's an amazing sculptress with a fantastic garden. She shares this big backyard space with several neighbors, and they were all thrilled to have the beehive there because they understand how important it is. I've asked so many people if I can put a hive in their yard, but they're afraid. Marsha was the first person who said emphatically, absolutely, *yes,* and she even has young children around because her daughter and family live in her home.

Most people just don't get it about bees; they're primally and irrationally afraid of them. I tell them they don't need to be afraid because honeybees are so busy they don't care about you; all they want to do is make babies and honey. They have to be really threatened in order to sting; if they sting they die, so it takes a lot for them to sting. I never hide that I'm a beekeeper; I want people to know and would rather have a confrontation with someone about bees so I can show them how safe and special they are and how important to nature.

When I set the box at Marsha's, I spent a long time trying to decide where I wanted it to go because of the flight path. We needed to place the opening in such a way that it wasn't a "bee line path," so to speak, because the public visits Marsha's garden, and we didn't want people walking through the flight path. Once the hive is set you can't move it—maybe an inch here or there, but the bees really hate it when you disturb the hive. We set the opening at an angle that was less direct so the bees would have to swoop down from above to enter; that way, instead of coming across the yard, they'd come down through the leaves into the hive.

We gave them a jar of honey water—half honey, half water—while they were getting acclimated to their new home. Marsha's is like a little resort; it's a magical oasis filled with amazing sculptures, trees, flowers, a koi pond and the world's most fantastic looking chickens. The hive was small, and we didn't know for sure if we got the queen, but I wanted to let them get acclimated before I looked extensively for her. When it felt right, I opened the box, took out the frames, and looked for her, but we never actually spotted her. When we did the extraction of another hive at Peter's, we took out two frames with honey and larvae from that one and replaced two in the new hive at Marsha's to strengthen it.

We had about five swarms last year from the one box. Marsha works at home and saw the swarm, which went into the blue bottle tree. It's a tree that doesn't leaf-out, and she had placed these gorgeous cobalt blue bottles on several of the branches. A colossal ball of bees landed on one of the bottles. I climbed up on an orchard ladder in my bee suit with gloves, a squirt bottle of sugar water and a smoker. I just grabbed the whole big mass of bees and put them in a big bucket.

Another swarm landed in a tree in Marsha's neighbor's yard. Again, I climbed up on a ladder, grabbed as many as possible, kept grabbing and grabbing, covered the bucket with a painter's sieve that has elastic on top, dropped them into the box and went back to get some more. I probably went back and forth four times until we were satisfied that we got the queen. Apparently we did.

THE BEEKEEPERS

A few months ago, we went through all forty frames and cut out the queen cells from the bottom two boxes. You do that so they won't swarm. If bees feel they're too crowded, they make a new queen and the old queen will take off with a group of bees, but they won't do that if there are no queen cells. So cutting out the queen cells is just a way to control the hive. We saw we had some happy, healthy bees with a lot of honey, so we put two supers on and encouraged bees to come up top by taking some of the frames most filled with honey and moving them up.

We also put several frames of honey and brood in the bottom box of the new hive (the one that we captured in the neighbor's yard). It's a very strong hive with lots of activity. There's a queen excluder between the top two and bottom two supers. Her Highness can't get up because she's too large to fit through, but the other bees can. We do that because if she were up in the top box she'd be laying brood and we wouldn't want to disturb the babies. We've thought about taking the excluder out because the queen is pretty ensconced in the bottom box, so I'm not sure we need it, and we don't think the other bees like it. There's plenty of honey in the one with the queen.

I think about the fact that the bees are still here in Marsha's yard after several years; that there are plenty of flowers for them to take pollen from. It's such a productive hive. Then, of course, I think about how we're going to get some honey this year, and I'm really excited about that. Urban honey is really good; it's a mixture of different flowers, like this great grenache of flowers from all over this area—lavender, salvias, oregano, sunflower, thyme, dahlias, nasturtium and star jasmine. There's a whole mishmash right here. I love urban honey's rich, multi-faceted, complex taste.

Keeping hives is a lot of work, but like gardening, I really love it. Part of it is the Zen of it. My job is so stressful as Director of After School Programs in Oakland that I love sitting and watching the bees, just like I love watering the garden. Bees are endlessly amazing and peaceful. My favorite thing is watching them fly in and out with different colored pollen on their legs—bright orange, bright yellow, bright red. I like to try to identify what flower the pollen's from.

Since my garden at home is so small and I can't get enough flowers to satisfy myself, I have a plot in a community garden nearby. I only grow flowers and only the flowers that the bees like: rosemary because it blooms so long, oregano and thyme, which is always just covered in bees. Everyone else there grows vegetables, and they realize how important the bees are; without them they wouldn't have any vegetables.

Someone had the poor idea to ask the city of Oakland if it would be fine to put a beehive in the garden and, of course, they said no. I said to tell the city we won't put a beehive in but there, but they should know there are hundreds and hundreds of bees in the garden anyway, so just beware.

This summer, I took a group of kids there because we had a program at the recreation center for students who are transitioning into middle school. The first day I was orienting them to the space, so I took them to the garden and showed them my plot and what I was growing. When I mentioned bees, they all looked around and started getting nervous. I said, "Notice they don't care that you're here; they're busy making honey. You have nothing to be afraid of." Suddenly a calm came over the whole group.

I'm still such a novice at beekeeping, but at least now I'm having success. I think it has to do with Marsha's great spirit. She's not only an incredible artist but a real chicken whisperer and bee whisperer. I love sitting here in the compost pile as her chickens climb on my lap for a pat, and just watching the bees. It's mesmerizing. They're coming back to the hive with pockets absolutely brimming with bright yellow pollen. I can see their wings are very healthy; if they were shriveled, it would be a sign of mites in the hive.

I've learned to be patient and not open the boxes at will like we did when I had the hive on my roof! Being a beekeeper involves mystery and patience, just like being a gardener. You plant this big homely brown bulb in the ground, and you think, is it really going to be like the picture shows? Then you wait and wait. With a hive, you set it up, and then stand back and let the bees establish themselves. You wonder how things are going in there but learn to enjoy watching them from the outside, speculating on their activity. Are we really going to get honey? The bees have been very busy all summer long, so we assume so. Soon enough, it'll be time to enter their inner sanctum and see.

At heart, I've always been an environmentalist so it's nice to be able to do something I enjoy that's also good for Oakland. Here in Oakland there are pockets of lushness that I'm sure have bees. One unsuspected pocket is a garden on 23rd Avenue in East Oakland where there's an enclave of young naturalists who keep an organic, sustainable garden. It's in an ugly location, right next to BART, but it's a gorgeous, amazing garden. They have a beehive that's a kind of Native American longhouse-looking structure and they've made slits for the bees to go in and out. Maybe the bees are more for pollination than harvesting honey, but I couldn't believe how many bees they had. I wouldn't have thought in East Oakland near the BART tracks there would be such successful honeybee hives and such a beautiful garden. Even on such a small scale things ripple out. I think more people should be keeping bees in their back yard or on their roof.

The Accidental Beekeepers
Pia & Jim Williams, Oakland

I guess we're about to become beekeepers. We have a huge double lot in the flats of Oakland with old fruit trees—several apple, pear, fig, plum, apricot, lemon, orange—and grape vines and blackberries. It's a perfect place for bees. We were cleaning out some of the brambles to give the fruit trees more room and found a huge feral beehive hanging from a branch in a willow tree just about three feet from the ground. It's about eighteen inches across and drops almost two feet into a gentle U curve; it looks like a huge heart. When there aren't thousands of bees on the surface—when many are out foraging—you can see five sheets of parallel comb. Each sheet is made of cells back to back, all with perfect hexagonal openings. The sheets are so organic looking and uneven, but still the surface is totally even with every hexagon the same size. The bees maintain the proportion of the hexagons no matter how the comb bends. They keep building comb up over the branch.

> Look at the three of us...we've been standing here watching the hive for almost an hour. I find them incredibly calming, like being mesmerized by the ocean.

It's been here quite a while now. We didn't notice it before we started clearing the thicket because we didn't see a steady stream of bees in a normal flight path. They had to weave their way through ten feet of willow branches. They must have had to make their way as an original swarm through all those branches of willow. Their flight path has changed since we opened up the branches.

THE BEEKEEPERS

We've decided to try to move them into a box hive because we want to take out the willow and free up the grape vines to make a grape arbor. Also, they'll be more protected when it rains. I doubt they've been there through the rainy season yet. It would also be great to get some honey. It's a challenge to figure out how to get them into the box, though. If we cut the branch, I'm sure the sawing would freak them out. One time we hit the branch slightly and we could see a ripple move through the whole hive. When we backed away the movement stopped. It's interesting...the swaying movement of the wind doesn't bother them, even a heavy wind, so either they know it's wind or they just don't perceive it as a threat of any kind. A sharp vibration is something unusual, and I'm sure a saw would be very threatening.

We've put our heads together with other beekeepers to come up with the least stressful way to get them into a box, one that doesn't hurt them and also makes them accept the box. We've decided we'll suit up, take a hot knife and slice through very slowly between the top of the hive and the branch and gently lower it down into two tall boxes. We'll figure a way to support it so it doesn't get crushed on the bottom. We'll set another box on top with frames and we might need to put in some drawn comb from another hive to make it smell like honey. We'll have to watch it carefully, because if they don't like it, they'll swarm. If we do it on, say, a Friday evening, since they don't travel around at night, we can watch really carefully on Saturday and Sunday when we're home and try to grab them if they take off.

Look at us...we've been standing here watching them for almost an hour. I find them incredibly calming, like being mesmerized by the ocean. You're on bee time when you watch them; they're doing something incredibly constructive, and a lot of their life is seemingly revealed to you. We can't see the inner workings, but you get an idea just from what you can see. It's as if they're sharing themselves with us. They'd be a little upset if we tried to harvest honey, of course, but just standing here watching them, practically in their line of flight, they're not bothered in the least. The hive is just amazing. When this was denser they probably could have gone through a rainy winter well covered by the thicket. With all their body heat they can keep it at a certain temperature.

It's not even like I expect something different to happen when I'm watching them. It's just interesting, and I get so absorbed that I have to consciously pull myself away. If I haven't seen the hive in a couple of days I have to come look. It's great in the morning...I walk the dogs at about 5:00 a.m., and I first check the hive. It's completely calm, not one bee flying yet. They're on the outside of the comb, and it's almost motionless.

***

A year later. We did attempt to put the bees in two deep hive bodies. Our fellow beekeeper Leah rigged it with twigs to support the hive, and then we cut the branch. When we put it in the boxes, it came apart. I watched for days as they carried out their dead but went on with their business. Almost three years later, they're thriving, whereas I'm not sure they would have made it through a winter once we exposed them to the elements by clearing their natural protection. We put a super on top of the deep hive, but they have no inclination to go up there to make comb. Consequently, we don't harvest any honey, but it's just nice having them here. We haven't opened the box for a few months now, and they are still very active. We will just let this hive live as is, since there is really no way to examine the individual combs. In the spring we will set up a new box for another colony — painted and ready to go — with proper frames for harvesting honey.

The Johnny Appleseed of Honeybees
Bill Tomaszewski, Marin Bee Co., Marin

About ten years ago, my wife Deb and I moved to California from New Jersey where I had been a police sergeant for twenty years. While I was working as a cop, Jersey City paid for me to go to law school, so I became a lawyer. I had a small practice during the day and worked nights as a cop. I had a friend nearby in Bernardsville who had a couple of beehives, which I always found interesting. I would have liked a few hives myself, but we didn't have the space.

When I retired from the police force and we moved here to Marin, finally we had enough space so I could try my hand at beekeeping. I started one hive, which I unintentionally killed three months later. I tried again the following year, and it was successful, so I felt confident enough to add another. I put a few more at my sister-in-law's home and tended them regularly.

Spending time around bees is utterly fascinating. The more hives you have, the more you notice the differences between them and what plants and flowers they forage for nectar and pollen. One hive can be smaller than the others, one a little weaker, some hives have bees who are noticeably more defensive, some are more laid back. I find the whole culture of the bees and what they do just fascinating, and the more I worked with them, the more

Will there be enough food on the planet?

This last question was foremost in our minds now that we were beekeepers and had become aware of the alarming rate at which honeybee colonies were mysteriously collapsing.

involved I got. It's amazing how they draw the comb out, how they raise their young, how they all have jobs to do from birth through death. Their first job is to take care of bees in the nursery, then they move to cleanup, then to building comb, then unloading the pollen, then security, then foraging...then they die. The whole hierarchy of their society and how they exist is amazing. Worker bees literally work themselves to death. A queen can live up to four years. Drones live for one season and then get kicked out of the hive to die in the cold after they've fulfilled their one purpose.

Debbie and I have always loved nature and the outdoors. As far back as I can remember we've had a garden full of vegetables and flowers and have spent as much time as our busy lives permit appreciating nature by walking, hiking and backpacking. While raising our children and thinking about their future, we felt an escalating concern for the world and its survival. We asked ourselves the inevitable and uncomfortable questions modern parents ask—what kind of a world will we leave our children? Will they even be able to breathe the air when they're our age? Will global warming kill off most species? Will there be enough food on the planet?

This last question was foremost in our minds now that we were beekeepers and had become aware of the alarming rate at which honeybee colonies were mysteriously collapsing. We knew they pollinate not only many fruits and vegetables, but also the grasses and clover that cows and other animals eat. We wanted to act on our growing concern for the world and its survival.

By last spring I had six or seven hives of my own and realized it was becoming an expensive hobby. I thought, how can I at least pay for this hobby? We had kept several thriving hives for years, giving away the precious raw honey. Friends and friends of friends began asking us to install hives, to buy our honey, or to buy equipment and bees. We realized we could make a difference and the time was right. The Marin Bee Company was our answer to both issues—supporting our intriguing hobby and contributing to repopulating bees. We'd save the world one bee at a time by installing beehives in community gardens, back yards and even on the grounds of corporations. Brilliant!

The first place I put a hive was at Mill Valley College and then we began to get requests throughout Mill Valley. I'd install the hives and either return to take care of them—checking for mites, disease, if they were getting ready to swarm, extracting honey—or teach people how to do it themselves.

Today I work as general counsel for Wine.com while Debbie runs Marin Bee Company. I'm an active person and I like being outdoors, working with my hands and working with the bees. I'm not the kind of lawyer who likes to sit at a desk and shuffle paperwork; I like to be out doing things, and this is a great avenue to get out and talk to people. I'm installing a hive on the roof of Wine.com's warehouse in Berkeley. The Chronicle contacted me and they may be putting a hive on the roof of their three-story building in San Francisco, where the garden section of the newspaper has its office.

I'm the official beekeeper for Google. This year they contacted me and I installed four beehives at their headquarters in Mountain View. Each is painted one of the Google colors—red, blue, yellow and green—and all are doing very well. They have employees who have adopted each hive. I've given seminars to the employees on beekeeping, one in the conference room and one hands-on outside at the hives. This fall I did a hands-on seminar on honey harvesting and extraction, and the employees who attended got to take home honey. It was well-attended, so obviously the beehives have been widely accepted.

For a corporation, beehiving can be a great thing for employees to work on cooperatively and can raise awareness of team building. My main goal is a sponsorship program where a corporation or person sponsors a whole hive or quarter of a hive, which is put in a community garden, a school garden or maybe on a farm or ranch. The hive is put there in the name of the corporation or individual, and I give them a certificate or a couple of bottles of honey, perhaps a video of the hives in action, so they have something tangible that shows they're actually sponsoring a hive. Sponsoring hives raises awareness of the plight of bees, and the more people we get to sponsor hives, the more bees can be spread throughout the country, or at least in the Bay Area.

Part of my overall purpose is to raise people's consciousness and give them, as a corporate entity, a bond amongst themselves with the bees. Honeybees have a lot in common with corporations; people have jobs to do like the bees, and all the bees work together for a common purpose much the same as all the workers in a corporation are working towards a common purpose. Companies are becoming more aware, more green, more environmentally concerned, and I think beekeeping goes hand in hand with that, helping give the corporation another avenue. The magic of keeping a beehive is that it's hands on, it takes you away from the stress of daily routines, it's a mental break for employees...it's transformative.

Another venue I'm very interested in is schools. We get a lot of calls to come talk to kids. Recently I got a call from Marin Learning Center, a preschool in Marin City, which is an anomaly in Marin County — a little pocket of poverty in the midst of one of the wealthiest counties in the country. They were looking for someone to talk to the kids and teach them about bees. My wife is a former schoolteacher, so she's the one who does presentations to school groups using our two-frame observation hive that kids find riveting. Raising children's consciousness about bees and how they play such a huge part in the food we eat is important.

THE BEEKEEPERS

I have over thirty hives of my own now, and I manage a bunch of others. One hive I've had for nine years, and I think those bees know me. They're super gentle and smart. I think they're well aware of their surroundings and what I do. I love to just watch them.

I want to be the Johnny Appleseed of honeybees. Honeybees have had a bad rap over the years and particularly hard times with Colony Collapse Disorder. I'm trying to make a difference, one bee and one person at a time.

Google's Hiveplex, Mountain View

The Engineer Beekeeper
Rob Peterson, Google

A little over a year ago, I had the idea of asking to keep honeybees at my place of work, Google. For me, the desire to keep honeybees was not only for personal reasons, but also because I wanted to raise people's awareness about the plight of the honeybee and felt it would be a wonderful group activity at Google. I'd wanted to keep bees for many years, but due to frequent moves and renting it didn't seem possible. Beekeeping has been in my family for several generations, so part of this interest has been there since I was a child. I grew up in Wales and had a couple of aunts who lived on farms where bees were part and parcel of the farming. I used to watch them tend the hives and was fascinated.

> I can't help but see the parallels between a hive and the way Google operates....A hive works seamlessly because every bee works for the whole, and it's expected that each individual will do their job to the best of their abilities.

Although I work at Google as a software development manager, I also have a degree in applied zoology and, as part of the course, studied the social insects in quite some detail, and this renewed my interest in becoming more intimately aware of the dynamics of the hive.

Google's an interesting place to work not only because there are so many people from diverse backgrounds, but also because of the work philosophy, which, to a very large degree, is based on trusting people to do "the right thing." Engineers are given a lot of flexibility to do their jobs with minimum supervision and are encouraged to work on their own projects one day a week. Google also recognizes the benefit of giving us the opportunity to do other things during the day, such as picking up a hobby, working on a personal project, or taking a class. Trusting us to do our jobs while having fun makes it a healthy environment to work in and, I believe, makes people more productive.

At Google, if you need anything to help you complete your work, you fill out a "help desk ticket." I filled one out requesting permission to have a few beehives; there was silence for weeks. A month later, I was put in touch with one of Google's chefs, Marc Rasic, whom I had never met before. Coincidently, he had initiated the process of acquiring beehives around the same time. and had already been in touch with Bill Tomaszewski of Marin Bee Company who brought us the hives and set them up.

When the email first went out that honeybees would be arriving at Google, the employees' overall reaction was very positive. We checked with Bill to make sure the bees were located in the right location with each hive painted in one of the four Google colors. It's a nice sheltered area with lots of sunlight. We have a sign saying, "Caution Bees at Work!" and we'll eventually put up informational signs. We have plans for a bee friendly garden. We want to educate people about the differences between honeybees, solitary bees, bumble bees, wasps, hornets, etc.

The honeybees fit right in with Google's commitment to sustainability. There are many solar panels on campus. We have a garden where we grow fruits, vegetables and herbs, and we have goats who "mow" the lawn and give milk. Now we have the bees as our resident pollinators.

Once the bees were set up in their hives, I sent an email saying that if anyone was interested in helping with them to let us know. We had many responses from people who wanted to be actively engaged in beekeeping. Since there were so many people, we decided to split into groups for each of the four hives, which has worked out very well.

Bill Tomaszewski has returned to give talks to employees about beekeeping and this fall did a hands-on class on extracting honey. There was a large turnout for the harvesting, which seemed to contribute to the camaraderie of sharing an interest and the sense of community around the bees. Generally our experience with the bees has been so positive that people in other offices were interested in beekeeping too.

I can't help but see the some parallels between a hive and the way Google operates. Google has a flat management structure. People are trusted to do the right thing in terms of their work and, in may respects, it's pretty well self-organized. A hive works seamlessly because every bee works for the whole, and it's expected that each individual will do their job to the best of their abilities.

The Chef Beekeeper
Marc Rasic, Google

My parents grew up in Croatia but moved to Luxemburg, which is where I grew up. We had a farm with a huge garden, our own chickens and always had bees. I grew up basically outside no matter the season because I was always intrigued by nature. I never had any fear about anything natural, so was always very comfortable around bees who were just an integral part of my day-to-day experience. I remember there used to be classes in beekeeping in the parks. Kids were always around, and nobody worried about them being stung, so they weren't taught fear. Generally kids in Europe are very natural with bees whereas here in the United States, everything is super protective, super processed. It's sad.

I thought about all the land here at Google and about how beehives don't take much space. They're easy to manage and not expensive. I wanted to do something to raise awareness of how bees are essential in terms of food production. I thought that by having bees around it would help lessen people's fear, plus I wanted to offer cooking classes using honey. My department is Workplace Services, which includes food and managing the real estate here. I do food program management, which means I run food service for part of the campus. I'm responsible for quite a few of the almost twenty restaurants and cafes and I organize food for childcare services. I went to my director, Dan Hoffman, and asked what he thought about keeping honeybees on campus. He was all for it, so I began the process of

> I wanted to do something to raise awareness of how bees are essential in terms of food production.

putting in a ticket. I had a budget that could pay for the hives, so finances weren't an issue. They hooked me up with Rob Peterson, we got the hives installed, and Rob went and bought veils, suits, smokers and other equipment.

The four hives—collectively known as the Hiveplex, of course—are each painted in one of Google's colors. We've placed them far enough away that anyone who isn't fond of bees can easily avoid them but close enough that anyone who wants to can walk over and watch them at work. Many Googlers have signed up to contribute to beekeeping and honey extraction efforts, and, come the harvest in the fall, we'll round the season off with a series of cooking classes and candle-making sessions. Honey's great to cook with if you know how to use it properly. You have to be careful not to heat it too much because excessive heat will kill the enzymes.

When we first put the hives up, there was an amazing waist-high field of wildflowers behind them, which was absolutely stunning. Unfortunately, it had to be cut down because it was a fire trap, but the bees solve these things. The marshes are near, so there are plenty of flowers there, lots on roadsides and even some scattered agricultural crops on the hill.

Beehives are organized similarly to how we do things here at Google. Bees have a flat management structure, and they adapt quickly and change roles throughout their career (nurse, guard, forager, quality controller, etc.) depending on demands. The bees that collect nectar from the forager bees at the entrance to the hive also scrutinize it for quality. If it's not high enough, they send the foragers back out to get a fresh start... it reminds me a bit of a Google code review!

If Google's a beehive, then I'm what you might call a forager. I work on the culinary team and we strive to serve food that's produced locally and grown in a sustainable manner. We wanted to take the effort to the next level. The hives contribute to our being as self-sufficient as possible.

THE BEEKEEPERS

***

On our recent fall extraction day, there was palpable excitement from the crowd of Googlers who watched as Bill Tomaszewski led us through the steps with the aid of a few volunteers. We harvested close to 450 pounds of honey, which has an exquisitely light, citrus flavor, and we put enough into mason jars for everyone involved in the Hiveplex to take some home. At the extraction I had a transformative experience when I finally summoned the courage to work with the bees bare-handed. It felt amazing to have hundreds of bees crawling all over my hands and feel no fear. They are very gentle creatures; they are beautiful.

Besides sustainability, self-sufficiency, raising awareness of honeybees and using honey to cook with, I had another reason for wanting to have beehives. I have a young son and want him to see that his father has done something really cool—establishing beehives in a big corporation. It's interesting and different. I haven't brought him down to the Hiveplex yet, but will when he gets older. I live in an apartment in San Francisco, so we don't have the luxury of being surrounded by countryside as I was as a child. Nature is very near and dear to my heart, and I thought hard about what to do for my son to expose him to nature. He's fascinated with honeybees. His first experience with a honeybee was catching one and getting stung. He did cry for a little bit but went straight back to observe them. Despite that experience, he's still very drawn to bees and continues to try to catch them on a flower so he can pet them. I love that. When a two-year-old doesn't have any fear, it's amazing. He thinks the honeybee is a beautiful animal.

The Physicist Beekeeper
Greg Robinson, Davis

I was one of the Hive Leads this past summer when I was interning at Google as a software engineer. I've been fascinated with honeybees for as long as I can remember and started keeping them a little over a year ago where I live in Davis while I'm studying physics at University of California, Davis.

I'm fascinated by the idea of honeybees' emergent behavior. They're very simple animals that as a group exhibit complicated behavior. I did a research project a while ago on what's called "particle swarm optimization," which sort of mimics bees foraging for nectar. Particle swarm optimization started as a model of flocking birds but turned out to be very useful for certain computational tasks. Optimization is a mathematical term that describes the process of finding a maximum or minimum for some function. Particle swarm optimization mimics the collective behavior of a colony of bees when they search for food in order to optimize some function. Bees want to maximize their ability to get nectar, so the optimum solution to their foraging behavior is that which optimizes the flow of nectar into the hive. Their activity can be approximated by considering each foraging worker as an individual agent that communicates with others. When one bee finds a source of nectar, she goes back to the hive and tells others. Those whom she tells will then be more likely to visit that location and tell more bees about it in turn. Particle swarm optimization models this strategy as a way to search for the optimum solution to an arbitrary function with many variables that

> I'm interested in why bees have such rich behavior. What are the underlying phenomena that give rise to that? I wouldn't say it's just instinct.

might be too complicated to sample completely.

I like to explain the natural world, so as a kid I was always that annoying guy who kept asking *why?* I'm interested in why bees have such rich behavior. What are the underlying phenomena that give rise to that? I wouldn't just say it's instinct. I don't believe in free will, which I believe is just an illusion. I even believe things like evolution are too abstracted in our minds, however true or predictive the ideas are. They spontaneously arise from simpler facts. In our world, everything relies on a single rule of physics and emergent dynamics comes from that. It's useful and interesting and productive to try to answer questions like why bees swarm in terms of evolutionary advantages. They happen to swarm because that's how they reproduce, so that's an easy one, but what causes them to *decide* to swarm? You can describe that in terms of pheromones, phase changes, etc., but that's only one level deeper and leaves more questions unanswered. I love studying that kind of thing.

Honeybees' instinct is not a separate entity. It's not some supernatural thing; instinct supervenes on physical facts. It's more interesting to me to explain their actions in terms of physical facts giving rise to it. I'm interested in the more complex behaviors of a large system, which depends on the simpler dynamics of individual, smaller systems. As applied to Google, each web page might not tell you a whole lot about its relevance to a search term, but looking at how they all interconnect gives you a lot more information. Partly because of that, deciding how to present the order of search results is a really complicated problem. When we're indexing and ranking pages on the internet, each page's content doesn't give you anywhere near the amount of information as the dependency graph of the links between them. From that bigger picture you can learn a lot more about how they relate, but this emerges from the simple properties of each individual page.

I do my hive inspections without gloves and wear a

tee shirt, never a bee suit and mostly without a veil. Today I wore a dark tee shirt, but I'll change it because bees don't like dark objects. Small patches of dark colors allegedly scare them. I go in without gloves for two reasons. One is that I get more tactile feedback when picking up the frames. I'm more aware of where my hands are, so I can bring out the frames more carefully. One scared bee can release pheromones that agitate the others. The other reason is it forces me to be gentler with the bees, because if you're gentle with them they're more likely to be nice to you. With my bees at home I don't even need a smoker because they're extremely mild. With the Google bees I use a little smoke, but they're also quite demure.

People are interested in being around bees mostly because they find bees fascinating creatures. Honey is quite a nice by-product but isn't the main reason to keep bees. I have bees because they're a constant learning experience. There's definitely a correlation between my study of physics, patterns, and looking to the natural world—very much including honeybees—to answer questions.

The Beekeeper & the Beekeeper's Wife
Spencer & Helene Marshall
Marshall's Farm, American Canyon

The Beekeeper: I was born in McMinnville, Oregon. My parents were both offspring of many generations of family farmers. If there was a crop to farm, I believe they farmed it. I know they at least farmed wheat and grain, raised turkeys and cattle. Grandma loved bees and had a few hives on their Yam Hill Farm. I remember watching her working the hives, and I was very curious. My family eventually moved to Acampo, near Lodi where they raised grains and started a harvesting business.

I moved away from the farm, went to college, and had various jobs teaching, gardening, producing videos and running a career development agency. My father was seriously injured in 1983, and I was needed to run the harvesting operations at the Acampo ranch. While I was living at the ranch, I started up a few beehives so I'd have something of my own to develop. I learned about beekeeping strictly by trial and error, and the more I learned, the more there was to learn.

> Basically, beekeeping hasn't changed very much for hundreds of years....but we're in a new ballgame now with all of the viruses and parasites.... The way we're doing it, folks, is not going to work anymore. We've got to change our ways.

Pollination is a big business in California's central valley. The almond crop is totally dependent on honeybees for pollination, and there was a need for more hives. I saw this as a good way to make enough money back then to pay for my slowly growing bee operation. I signed a few pollination contracts and started moving my bees to the almond groves, the cherry and apple orchards and the clover fields of the San Joaquin Valley. I used money earned from pollination to buy used equipment and hives from beekeepers who were giving up beekeeping, and this is how I began to develop apiaries in several locations. I alternated between taking care of my dad, running the business and doing carpentry and remodeling jobs. The bees, however, became an obsession. I wasn't happy just having bees in the Central Valley; to satisfy my yearning, I started up a few hives in Marin County where I lived.

The Beekeeper's Wife. I'm a city girl, born and raised in San Francisco. The last thing I ever thought would happen to me would be to have a beekeeper for a husband. I had studied art and sculpture at Berkeley and had been introduced to bees and beekeeping by a forestry professor at UC Berkeley. I had moved to the East Coast where there was always a beehive in my yard, but I was not a beekeeper. I decided to move my family and my business back to California and bought a commercial building on Sir Francis Drake Boulevard in Marin to be the home of my art-chime business. A year after I moved, a mutual friend introduced me and Spencer, telling me beforehand that he was a beekeeper. When we met, the first thing I asked him was, "Do you have Italians or Carniolans?" " Carniolans," he said…and that was the beginning of a sweet relationship and Marshall's Farm as we know it today.

The Beekeeper: At the time we met, I was dreaming about doing farmers' markets to sell my honey. Helene had been in the gift business doing craft fairs and gift shows in all the big cities for so long that doing a farmers' market didn't seem like such a big deal. She thought it would be a lot of fun.

One day, by accident, I left a hive full of bees in Helene's van. She was going to a craft fair to sell her chimes near Placerville. When she got there, she found the hive (not

THE BEEKEEPERS

yet buzzing) and a bucket full of canning jars filled with honey. She set the hive out as part of her display and put the honey out — for sale — next to the hives. As the day heated up, the bees buzzed, signaling they were getting ready to go forage, and she put the hive back in the van. She sold $20 worth of honey that day and drove back to the ranch with a van-full of flying, buzzing bees. I greeted her, probably with a smirk on my face. She said, "Here's some money, honey!"

The Beekeeper's Wife: Spencer is a passionate beekeeper. He loves to mess around with bees. There's nothing that makes him happier than sticking his head or bare hands into a beehive. He manages the hives, and I manage the business doing sales and marketing, designing labels, packaging and brochures and managing the finances. I've always run my own small business, and I love it. We're totally opposite from each other — a perfect match!

What we've accomplished takes two different personalities to work the different aspects of our business. As I say, he gets the honey; I get the money. We've been married for a long time now. We work together, we live together, but we're each doing our own thing within one superstructure, so to speak. Kind of like a mini-beehive. He's doing what he's passionate about; I'm doing what I'm passionate about, but one without the other, this honey business wouldn't have happened.

There are so many beekeepers who are just into pollination of mono-crops or producing drums of honey, whereas we're bringing local urban honey to the public in a way that they normally wouldn't be able to get it. Our honey is in specialty grocery stores and local farmers' markets and used by many upscale restaurants and celebrity chefs, but we also ship all over the country.

The Beekeeper: We have a hand-crafted approach to traditional honey production. We specialize in local honey, harvesting small quantities of superior quality honey in the very special microclimates of the San Francisco Bay Area. Much of our honey is wildflower, but we also produce many different varietals. I search out locations that support only a few hives but produce exceptional tasting honeys. The diverse and constantly changing seasonal blooms of the Bay Area — eucalyptus, star thistle, wild blackberry, sage, orange and others — produce nectars and pollens that differ greatly in taste, texture and color. I harvest after each bloom, isolate the honey harvested from each apiary, and thus create the special flavored nuances and wonderful color variations in our honey.

The Beekeeper's Wife. Our business specializes in artisanal production, and we're very proud of it. We're very low tech. We're not using a lot of power. In the honey house, we have only two pieces of electric equipment, the uncapper and the extractor. Everything else is done by hand. All the bottling is done one jar at a time — filling it with honey, labeling it. There's no assembly line here, and that way we can bring small quantities of a large variety to our honey fans. The honey's real — no additives and unfiltered. It is certified Kosher — the ultimate symbol of purity. If you look closely, you can see natural pollen particles floating in the honey. Honey is a healing, healthful, fat-free food with minerals and vitamins. We use it every day — in tea, on toast, in baking, in dressings, marinades and sauces and on salads, fruits, veggies and meats. It's great as a sweetener and flavor enhancer, and even better right out of the jar.

The Beekeeper: Basically, beekeeping hasn't changed very much for hundreds of years, other than the invention of extractors and uncappers and things like that. If you've got a certain amount of knowledge, you can survive. We're in a new ballgame now with all of the viruses and parasites, so you have to stay on top of it. There are some scientific journals that come out every month, which I read from cover to cover and talk to other beekeepers about what they're doing. The way we're doing it, folks, is not going to work anymore. We've got to change our ways.

Recently we installed some hives on the roof of the Fairmont Hotel in San Francisco. I love that they're bringing awareness of the plight of the honeybees to the public. It's crucial to get people involved in understanding how important honeybees and all the other pollinators are to our survival.

The Beekeeper's Wife: I jumped at the invitation to put hives at The Fairmont. I spent many nights after high school proms and parties at The Fairmont, exactly where our hives are now.

The Beekeeper: We have a lot of problems in this country and in the world. People are still like children; we haven't really woken up to our full potential or what we should be doing. I think being an adult means taking care of business, being smart in how you interact with the world, and building a social network with people. If you find something that you love to do and it's a positive thing in the world, do it in a smart, positive way. That's what I feel I'm doing in my beekeeping and I'm grateful for being able to work at something I love.

A good friend of ours described my typical day: "He takes the bees to the flowers in an air-conditioned SUV (it's air-conditioned because it's a flat-bed truck!). When the bees are finished working the chosen flowers, he whistles to gather them up and bring them home! Now there's a great day at work!"

The Honeybees of Nob Hill
Chef JW Foster, The Fairmont Hotel, San Francisco

This past summer 80,000 honeybees were invited to take up residence at the best address in San Francisco—The Fairmont Hotel, Nob Hill. They don't pay rent, but they do a great service pollinating our new culinary garden and giving us honey. We're delighted to have them.

Many people have a deep connection to this hotel and now the bees are adding to that. This elegant Beaux-Arts landmark survived the earthquake of 1906 but was ravaged by fires inside. Architect/engineer Julia Morgan oversaw the Fairmont's renovation, hired because of her pioneering use of reinforced concrete to insure its survival in another earthquake. Time and again I hear people say things like, "My grandmother brought me here for afternoon tea when I was a child;" or, "I spent my honeymoon here...."

> The cooks come out to the garden to cut the herbs, which gives guests a chance to interact with them and also see the bees coming and going, landing on the herbs that will land in their dinner.

I arrived at the Fairmont only a few months before the honeybees. I had trained as a chef in Toronto and worked at several country inns up until about ten years ago. At that point I decided I wanted to try cooking in hotels and see what they had to offer. I worked at the Royal York in Toronto and then the Fairmont Dallas, which is when I got interested in honeybees. My wife and I were at the local farmer's market and we ran into a gentleman dressed in a bee costume. I don't mean the white bee suit that a beekeeper wears; this was a real costume—yellow and black with antennae bobbing on his head. First I walked by and thought, that's a little odd...but, to each his own. He was selling honey and had a glass observation hive. I went back the next weekend and started talking to him; he was so passionate, telling me about what was going on with honeybees, how much trouble they're in and why we need them. I'm always fascinated with people who really love what they do and take it to that driven level. Here he is in a bee costume to attract people so he can chat with them. I listened to him in awe and began the process of installing hives at the Fairmont Dallas.

It took me awhile to get to the Fairmont San Francisco, but it was well worth the journey. I love San Francisco; it's an amazing playground for a chef. You couldn't ask for a better place to cook—all the restaurants and markets and fresh produce—it's all right here, and I'm totally enjoying it.

When I first arrived, I was walking in the hotel and saw the perfect spot to have beehives. There's a large roof in the back of the hotel that's easily accessed from the foyer leading to the Pavilion Room. I asked a couple of purveyors of local produce who the local bee farmer was. One guy looked at me a little strangely, but I said, "Can you just put me in touch? I've got an idea."

First he thought I was joking, but then he told me about Helene and Spencer Marshall of Marshall's Farm. They manage hives all over the Bay Area and produce wonderful honey. I got in touch with them and it became a great partnership because they really love the Fairmont and, of course, they love honeybees.

I wasn't surprised when the San Francisco management completely embraced the idea of having bees here. There are bees at Fairmonts not only in Dallas, but in Washington, D.C., Canada, China and Kenya. The Fairmont has long had a reputation for concern about environmental issues and has always been a leader in the hotel industry. All our new buildings are green certified, all our hotels recycle, and whenever there's a possibility to put a garden in one of our buildings, we take advantage of that. So the Fairmont is very forward thinking about what needs to be done for the community and the environment. It's the fabric of who we are at the Fairmont to be authentically local and responsible to the community.

I've always held that belief. Coming from country inns, as a chef you're automatically connected with local farmers. They come in the back door to offer their produce, and you get to see how passionate they are. I love that, and am forging partnerships with local growers here. I always think about how we can build a partnership, and what we can offer our guests that's unique that they can't get anywhere else.

Now I get phone calls all the time from local farmers who are hearing about us. Yesterday someone called saying, "I have 150 pounds of heirloom tomatoes that need to be used. Would you be interested?" So a pick-up came to the back of the hotel that afternoon with bushels of the most gorgeous tomatoes.

The Marshalls set up four hives. They come weekly to check them and do the honey extractions. We planted several beds of lavender for when the bees first arrived so they'd have something to grab, and they've been feeding quite regularly on that. They also fly off and forage elsewhere. Their flight path seems to be shooting straight out in the direction of the Bay Bridge, and I'm sure they're finding plenty in all the rooftop gardens in the area. There are lots of small water fountains for them to drink from, and some like to go to the penthouse for a drink. You can't blame them; I would, too.

The rest of the beds will soon be filled with more culinary herbs—rosemary, thyme, oregano basil, chives, cilantro—whatever we can use in the kitchen. The bees will have a heyday with those herbs. It will be a very functional garden, not ornamental. The cooks will come out to the garden to cut the herbs, which will give guests a chance to interact

THE BEEKEEPERS

with them and also see the bees coming and going, landing on the herbs that will land in their dinner. It's exciting because many of our guests are very much engaged with the bees. They've heard about them and want to see them. One of the first things many people ask when they arrive at the Fairmont is, "Where are the bees?" The buzz is out on the streets of San Francisco!

Guests appreciate that we're sustainable in our practices and use local, organic produce. There's so much interest these days in how food gets from the field to the plate, and people are coming in hungry to experience what's local. San Francisco is a great city for this because so many people understand the principles behind eating local, sustainable food. It's not a fad; it's just part of the fabric of the culinary rubric here.

As a chef, I think it's important to support this. The more people are aware of what we're eating, where food actually comes from, who's raising it, and what we need to do to help the environment contributes to more solutions. The fish we serve in this hotel is fresh off the pole and has got to be green; it cannot be on any endangered list. We're bringing in grass-fed meats, and now we're giving these honeybee gals a nice place to live; in turn, we appreciate their pollinating services. We're going to build a several-acres Fairmont Farm out in Petaluma where we'll grow unusual organic vegetables for the restaurant, which will fit in nicely.

After only four months we were able to harvest two supers of honey, which is quite a bit for such a short time. I use the honey in many ways—sorbets, ice creams, in our dressings, in breads. We'll bottle it as well. We're even thinking about a beer made out of our honey. This might be the only place in town to serve honey beer!

Honey is beautiful. Since I've been here, we're getting away from using plain sugar and sweeteners and going towards the honey, which we serve with our afternoon tea. We use honey it in its most natural state, leaving it alone as much as possible so the lavender or whatever taste is experienced. We do mostly cold cooking, only a little bit of hot, but not much, because cooking honey at too high a temperature kills the enzymes. If we use it in a brioche, we usually just baste the top at the end so it soaks in a bit.

What's great about having honeybees at the Fairmont is that we have an opportunity to educate people about how important bees are. Guests are everywhere, and nobody's screaming and running away because of the bees. In fact, people actively seek them out. Housekeepers, guests and colleagues like to come into the kitchen and tell me, "Wow, the bees are just flying around out there." I see people with their face pressed against the window looking out at the culinary garden and the bees. Sometimes I look up and see people staring out of their rooms at everything going on on the roof. Our banquet room has windows out to the terrace, and I get comments about how guests are walking over and staring at the bees while a meeting is going on. I try to get people who are afraid of bees to come out on the roof and look at the hives from a few yards away. It's funny how much they relax when they realize the bees don't want to hurt them, and that there's nothing to fear. I especially love that children seem so interested. When they come to the hotel we talk about food, and I introduce them to the bees and the gardens. It's great to get them at that age to really understand bees and how intertwined their future is with the future of bees.

Honeybees totally surround what I love to do for a living. As a chef, I feel a responsibility to my industry, and in addition as a human being, I feel a responsibility to help the honeybees who are in bad shape. It's been going on for years and doesn't seem to be getting any better. I don't think enough people realize the role honeybees play in the scheme of things, and that without them, we're in serious trouble. Whenever I get an opportunity to show people the garden and tell them about the bees, I'm thankful. If it helps talking to a chef and my passion comes out about what I love to do, then I'll just keep being a spokesperson.

Bees have been on this planet far longer than we have and have never needed us before. We've upset the balance so much that now they need us as much as we need them. Let's support them and get their numbers back up; let's find out what the issues are so that we can move forward for all of us before it's too late.

Our Pollen Princesses
Michael Cooper and Deno Marcum, San Francisco

When I announced to Deno that we were getting bees he wasn't particularly excited but was definitely not disinterested. Coming from a food background, he was intrigued on that level. I, on the other hand, have always thought bees were fascinating creatures—the colony mentality, the way they have a community to maintain themselves and solve problems. I got interested in actually keeping bees about four years ago when the general public was beginning to be commonly aware of Colony Collapse Disorder. Nobody really understood what was causing it, and unfortunately, they still don't, although there are several theories. I did a lot of browsing around on line trying to find more information about Colony Collapse and came across a website on the "hobby beekeeper." With a little more research I realized beekeeping was something I could do.

> San Francisco is very supportive of backyard agriculture....There are actually quite a few thriving backyard farming operations— vegetable gardens, chickens, bees. If you've got enough room, as long as it's not a nuisance to your neighbors or violating health codes, it's fine.

I spent time ahead studying to make sure I understood what the bees required and what I'd need to do to keep the colonies happy and healthy, not to mention keep them from bothering our neighbors. It's okay to keep bees in San Francisco, which surprised me when I first started looking into it. Actually it's not just allowed, but encouraged. The more I talked with beekeepers in the area and learned

THE BEEKEEPERS

about "urban agriculture," I found that San Francisco is very supportive of backyard agriculture and apparently always has been. There are actually quite a few thriving backyard farming operations—organic vegetable gardens, chickens, bees. If you've got enough room, as long as it's not a nuisance to your neighbors or violating health codes, it's fine.

I got the bees plus all the equipment on line. Our housemate wasn't thrilled when he got home and there was a buzzing box at the top of the stairs. We wondered what the mail person thought about delivering bees; maybe he or she is used to it by now.

The bees came in a little wire cage box, open on two sides—three pounds of bees and some sugar water for them to eat in transit. The queen was in her own little compartment with the entrance plugged by sugar paste. We set up all the equipment and just dumped the bees into the hive rather unceremoniously. The queen, still in her cage, was then suspended between two frames and the hive was closed up. The other bees ate the sugar paste over the next couple of days until Her Highness was released and joined the hive. During this time the rest of the bees had become accustomed to her scent and accepted her as their new queen.

At first we set up the hive in our back yard. We live in a relatively small Edwardian apartment building in a little neighborhood in Noe Valley. The building has nine units—each a full flat—so we have our own front and back entrance and since the building takes up three lots, there's a large shared back yard. Most of the other residents weren't spending much time in the back yard so Deno and I sort of took it over. It was all weeds and we cleaned it up. When a family with some very rambunctious children moved, in we decided to move the colony to a friend's back yard several blocks away. Although bees are gentle when undisturbed, you can't expect children to stay out of their flight path and we figured it was better for both the bees and the children to remove the bees. They seem happy in their current yard.

Eventually we had two hives in that yard and two more on the roof of Bi-Rite Market just off Dolores Park and 18th Street. Deno and I have a few foodie friends who work at Bi-Rite and we were talking one day about whether we could place some honey with them. We were also looking for a new place to put some hives, and they suggested the roof of the market. We ran to the roof, and it looked great so we put a couple of hives there. We tend the bees, and the market has first dibs on the honey that comes out of that. They purchase it and put their own label on — Rooftop Honey.

We just recently set up another hive on the roof of another friend's apartment. It's been a rough year for our colonies. Two have died and one's struggling. The other two are healthy. One died from a particularly heavy case of nosema, which is to bees what the flu is to us — a stomach virus. It got to the point where they just weren't a strong enough population. Even if you catch it early, there's only a 50% chance of survival. Sometimes the bees weather it just fine if they get a good supply of nectar going and the weather warms up, but in this hive it got too thick too early in the year.

Another hive was infected with foulbrood, a particularly virulent disease affecting the larvae. We had to first determine whether it was European or American foulbrood. European can often be cured, but American foulbrood can only be dealt with by destroying the colony so there can be no risk of contagion to nearby colonies. After finding that it was European, we tried to rescue that colony by basically quarantining all the adult bees and starving them for a few days so their intestines could clean out. Then we put them in a whole new box with sugar water. They lose all the wax they've built and start anew. They seemed to be limping along, the queen was starting to lay new eggs, and the population was beginning to build back a little when all of a sudden they absconded from the hive. I don't know if it was the result of the disease or if it was Colony Collapse Disorder, which we had never experienced before. In this case the hive had a lot of the same symptoms of CCD, but since they were recovering from foulbrood, it's hard to tell. Research hasn't really pinpointed the cause of CCD yet. They have some leads, but nothing conclusive yet.

So we only have three hives at the moment. We still have some honey left from our final harvest last year that we haven't sold. Last year was actually a good year for us. Four of the five hives did quite well, and we ended up with 300 pounds of honey, which is an enormous amount. The second year we had just the one hive and got 140 pounds. They can be really productive if everything is working in their favor.

We have a little online shop for people who are unable to shop at Bi-Rite, but that's just a little pin money. It's a hobby, but not a full scale business because we both have regular jobs. We came up with the name Pollen Princesses when we were batting around ideas. I'm a huge fan of alliteration to begin with, and we had been thinking about the fact that every worker in the hive is a daughter of the queen, so that makes them all princesses.

We do the honey extraction in our kitchen. We check out the equipment from the local beekeepers' association, usually getting a pretty large extractor with an electronic motor that can comfortably extract six frames of honey at a time. It comes apart, so we lug it home and put it back together in the kitchen. We carry the frames in a plastic lined box from the hive to our house by bus, which causes a lot of interaction with our bus mates. When it's time to harvest, we buy bottles on line, sterilize them in our sink and fill them up with the beautiful honey. After a few extractions, we'll have people over for honey tastings.

What amazes me is how wildly different one extraction can be from the next, based on what flowers are available at certain times and where the bees decide to forage. Even if we extract from hives that were side by side we'll find the flavors very different. Clearly, each group has been foraging on different plants even though they return to hives that are only inches apart. We assume they're going to different places because of the way the honey tastes. Bees often forage up to four miles, but usually they stay within one or two miles. One of the things about San Francisco is the bees have a pretty broad range of flowers, unlike bees farther out in the country where their hive might be in a field of all the same plant. If they go to Golden Gate Park they're going to come across totally different flowers than if they go forage in back yards of Bernal Heights.

We don't have any way of determining what flowers the bees were foraging, so we can't specify that our honey is lavender or orange or anything like that. We just call it wildflower. We do up to six extractions; if we did just one or two extractions, we'd get all the honey produced during the year, and it would be very general wildflower. We want to maintain the separation from batch to batch, so we meticulously keep each extraction separate and label the jars with the extraction date. If someone's interested they can count back a month or six weeks to figure what would have been in bloom in their neighborhood to get an idea of what flowers might be blended into that honey. People love the idea of local honey reflecting the flavor their neighborhood; it makes it more intimate.

It's fascinating to us to see how the flavor changes so much. Sometimes you can pick out a distinct flavor—oh, that tastes exactly like the Victoria Box was in bloom. Or on one particular date you're going to get honey with really sweet floral notes, which will go well with tea; or this honey is much darker in color and a little more syrupy in consistency; it has earthy, herbal overtones. We even had one that had a distinctive mint taste. One was a little grassy in flavor and dark green, which was unusual. It smelled of California lilac amongst other things. Sweet, but not cloying.

Another thing I find interesting is that people buy our honey because they believe local honey is good for their allergies. I don't know that we've had anyone come back and say their allergies are improved or cured, and I'm not sure there's any conclusive evidence that pollen found in local honey mitigates allergies. I do give that idea some credence, however, and a lot of our customers do also, so for them if their allergies are worse during certain months, they should get honey collected from that month. It certainly can't hurt.

This was our fourth season. Last year we had six harvests, but this year we only had two because it was a very cold winter, and the hives had some setbacks. The honey was just what was available at the end of the season. We knew when it was time to harvest by looking into the supers to see how full they were. We were careful, as always, to leave plenty for our princesses to winter-over comfortably.

Any time I see a honeybee within a mile of our hive, I wonder if it's one of our princesses. I wish her happy foraging, full pockets and safe return to her colony.

The Lost Art of Bee Tracking
Tom Manger, Pleasanton

My family and I are beekeepers. Besides having hives, my oldest daughter and I are hoping to revive the lost art of bee tracking. She likes doing it because it has all the components of an adventure—the quest, knowledge and understanding of the "hunted" and bit of patience and tenacity. I love it because it's a great activity to do together, and it teaches my daughter about bees and how to gently track an animal, purely out of curiosity.

In ancient times, honey was the only available sweetener and beeswax was a prized commodity. Bee hunting was a commercial endeavor that invariably ended with the destruction of the hive resulting from the removal of all honey and wax comb from the colony. Nowadays, modern beekeeping techniques have made it possible to harvest both wax and honey without harming the colony or their nest. So, bee hunting is largely a lost art.

> ...in the back of our minds there's the hope that our tracking and cataloging of feral colonies in our area might contribute worthwhile data on the overall health of bees.

It's not necessary anymore to satisfy one's sweet tooth. We do it for the pure joy of seeing where honeybees might have a nest. And, in the back of our minds there's the hope that our tracking and cataloging of feral colonies in our area might contribute worthwhile data on the overall health of bees.

When foraging honeybees finish filling their stomachs with nectar and/or finish filling their pollen baskets with pollen, they head back to their colony in the most direct route possible. They make a "bee line" back to their hive. It's this one fact that makes bee hunting (aka beelining) possible. Whereas it's possible to watch the flight behavior of random bees in the hope of seeing one head from a foraging area straight back to her nest, this is hardly an efficient use of time because the typical bee needs a full hour and several thousand flower visits before filling up and returning to her nest. So, to speed up the process bee trackers provide the bees with sugar water so they'll quickly fill up their stomachs and return to their colony in just a matter of minutes.

Foraging honeybees share good sources of nectar and pollen. So, upon returning to the colony a worker bee will do a "waggle dance" to communicate the direction and distance of the new food source. The recruited bees then venture to the same spot to help ferry the loads of bounty back to the colony.

Sometimes my daughter and I just do simple tracking with a bait station filled with honey. We set out our container and wait for honeybees to find it. Once a few bees have found the treat, they'll recruit others to help ferry the food back to their nest. With lots of bees going back and forth between the bait station and their nest, we can visualize a bee line that gives us the general direction of their nest. We then move the container of honey a few hundred feet further along the bee line and wait for the bees to come drink. We repeat this process with additional bait stations further down the bee line. The closer we get to their nest, the faster recruited bees come to the bait station and the faster we're able to establish the next leg of the bee line. Thus we leapfrog the bees to the nest. This is the traditional "passive" technique for bee tracking.

It's an easy transition from passive bee tracking to "active" bee tracking. This is when we capture foraging bees (briefly) in a jar and conscript them to take our sugar water. This eliminates the unknown amount of time involved when setting out a bait station and waiting for the first batch of bees to show up.

Honeybees use the polarization of sunlight to navigate to and from their nest. So, when they are in an enclosed space, they will instinctively fly towards the brightest source of light. Instead of using a cardboard or wooden box to capture honeybees, we use a clear container so they will fly upwards toward the light to try to escape. We like to use a clear glass jar and lower it over the bee as it feeds on a flower. We then bring the lid up from below to cut off the bee's escape. When the bee flies to the top of the jar, we can remove the lid long enough to move the jar up and away to prevent damage to the flower.

We move the bee in the jar to the bait station, remove the lid and place the jar on top of the bait station so the bee can get to it without drowning (i.e. bees don't swim well, so they need something to land on). With the jar on top of the bait station, the bee will still be furiously beating her wings trying to fly away, so she needs to be calmed down. We cover the jar with a dark cloth so no light is visible. Without light, she'll stop flying, land on the bait station and start filling her stomach with sugar water. After a few minutes, we remove the cover and let the bee fly away.

We continue capturing and conscripting bees to the bait station. But, once they start making return trips from their hive to the bait station, our work is done. The first conscripts have recruited other bees on our behalf. (It's the insect version of multi-level marketing but without the sales pitch!) We conscript just a few bees, and they'll get dozens more involved in a reasonably short order.

At this point, we have our bee line established and can move our original bait station down the beeline. Or, we can just create a second, third, and fourth bait station further down the bee line. Any way we do it, we'll leapfrog closer and closer to their colony.

In the old days of bee hunting, there were wide open swaths of land. The bee hunter could tramp across miles without coming across a single man-made barrier. This is rarely possible nowadays, and in an urban/suburban environment you can't go more than a few hundred feet before you start trespassing on someone's property. Using a GPS allows a bee hunter to continue walking an established bee line after circumnavigating an obstruction. This saves a lot of effort and lost time in a suburban area. It also allows a bee hunter to discontinue a hunt, then pick up the trail at a later date.

Knowing the last known tracking position is easy in an urban environment (corner of 5th and Willow). But, should you venture into the woods or other open spaces, the way points are not easy to reestablish without cairns or other markers. Setting your last known location as a way point in your GPS makes it easy to get back on the hunt.

GPS technology certainly isn't needed to track bees. Rather, it is a fun add-on to the experience. For me, it is a way to teach my daughter about GPS, mapping techniques and geographic information systems. What child doesn't want to know about this stuff? For today's youth, technology is an ingrained part of their lives. For my own kids, I like to teach both the old and new ways to accomplish the same task.

First Swarm
Bill Hoskins, Orinda

Going out to catch a swarm is often an unexpected urban adventure. To get swarm calls we started by putting our name on the beekeeper list maintained by the fire and police departments, SPCA, agriculture department and the San Francisco Beekeepers Club. The first swarm I responded to was on a telephone pole at a busy intersection. When I arrived it looked like the scene of a major accident with two fire trucks, three police cars, and a local TV station keeping their distance from the bees. I was a sixteen-year-old kid coming in to save the public from this hazard that the police and fire fighters couldn't handle. However, I had never actually hived a swarm before. My knowledge came from reading an article in "The American Bee Journal" about how to do it. I was convinced that it was actually easy and that the true risk of getting stung was almost zero when bees are swarming. Even though I was a complete novice, I certainly looked the part with a bee veil, small broom to sweep bees and a cardboard box. I didn't let on that this was my first time. I was determined to look very professional for the TV camera.

I balanced the ladder against the pole and climbed up eighteen feet to the bees. Following the instructions I had read, I brushed all of them into the box. When the bees fell into the box something happened that completely surprised me. They were actually heavy, and the weight of the bees

> The bees were successfully in the box, but I was now precariously clinging to the pole with a ladder dangling off to the side, held from falling by my legs.

upset the balance of the ladder on the pole. (The article had not mentioned that a really big swarm with 25,000 bees can weigh twelve pounds or more due to their being engorged with honey for their journey.) Fortunately, I was able to throw my arms around the pole to keep the ladder from falling without dropping the box of bees. So much for looking professional for the TV camera! The bees were successfully in the box, but I was now precariously clinging to the pole with a ladder dangling off to the side held from falling by my legs. I was unable to pull the ladder back onto the pole, and both my arms were needed to hold the pole and the box of bees. I was hopelessly stuck, and of course the camera was still rolling, and the crowd of spectators was growing.

    I called to the police and fire fighters that I needed some help. The policeman in charge said that they couldn't help because they would get stung. I responded that they wouldn't sting, that I was not wearing gloves, and they weren't stinging my hands. At that point one of the policemen volunteered to his superior to help me out. He straightened the ladder for me and held it as I climbed down with a small cloud of bees swarming about the box. I set the box on the ground, and the TV came in for a close-up. They interviewed me about bees and beekeeping in San Francisco. When they asked about how long I had been collecting swarms, I said that my father and grandfather had been keeping bees off and on for several years. I never mentioned that this was my very first swarm. That night KRON TV reported on the story. I was quite relieved that they didn't show the part where I was holding on to the telephone pole for dear life with the ladder dangling and bees buzzing. In fact, they closed the piece with the warning that "if you see a swarm of bees like this, let the experts handle it because they have many years of experience."

Urban Farmer & Beekeeper
Mauro Correa, Oakland

Alice's Wonderland Urban Farm, named by my daughter, is our one-acre mini farm right in the center of Oakland. My wife and I had been living in San Francisco but longed for a garden, so we began looking on this side of the Bay. Although we hadn't thought of something this large, when we saw the land, we loved it. It's unusual, and must be what Oakland was like decades ago—small, self-supporting family farms. When we first moved in about nine years ago it was nothing but dried grasses, overgrown blackberry bushes and fennel. Now we have fruit trees, many vegetables and herbs, native plants and flowers, chickens and ducks for eggs and bees for pollination and honey.

> In nature, bees will try to make a hive that's round. If they are inside a tree they follow the form of the trunk. In the box, we want them to build the frame straight because it's easy to get the honey out.

I'm a classical musician from Brazil but I moved to the Bay Area in 1997. When my daughter was born, I started playing Brazilian jazz at restaurants and nightclubs so I could take care of her in the day while my wife worked. I used to sell my produce at great prices to the same restaurants I played in. I still gig but very little now because so many places have closed since the economy fell. Now I sell my extra produce to the neighborhood.

The first year we lived here we had swarm after swarm of honeybees, especially in the spring. The neighborhood bees probably thought this was a good place to live because of the extensive gardens. I called a beekeeper who has become a friend, and she'd come pick up the swarms, but more kept coming. When one moved into the extra building on the property I thought, *Okay, I'm just going to start keeping bees.* I got the equipment and a little how-to book, and just as I had begun the garden by teaching myself, I started the hives.

I have a pretty natural philosophy about beekeeping. I don't bother the bees much, I don't medicate them, and I keep their hives small. I let all my vegetables go to seed so they have pollen and nectar when the seeds take root. My beekeeping style is not the most profitable, but I don't care about that. They give me so much—the pollination of my garden and the honey itself, which is all the sugar my family and I eat. This year I probably got 100-150 pounds out of only three hives. If I have more than we need, I sell it to people in my neighborhood.

Every time a beekeeper goes into the hive it's an invasion, and even if you are really careful, you inevitably smash a few bees. Many beekeepers go into their hives a lot because they want to check on the queen, to see if she's laying brood, and also to clean the hive. I let the bees be. I check on them every three to four weeks to a month depending on the strength of the hive. If I know they're really strong and making a lot of honey, I check them more often so I'll know when to put a super on.

I keep the hives small because if honeybees have space, they just keep filling it and growing. When I take a little of their honey, it gives them some space to work and they make a little more, but they don't need to increase their hive because I haven't given them lots more room.

I never medicate for mites or other problems. If they have a problem, it's the same as they would have in the wild. I use a screen on the bottom of the hive to deal with mites. Normally the mites come in on the bee's legs, and they'll fall to the floor, so if there's no floor, they'll fall through the screen to the ground and they can't come up. A lot of people use wooden boards and I suspect they have more problems with mites, which I haven't had ever since I started using the screens. Screens also help to ventilate the hive.

I've always loved nature. When I was a young boy, I used to spend days camping alone in the woods. I have a deep empathy and love for animals, which has made me a vegetarian for more than thirty years. For me, it just didn't make any sense to eat meat. I meditate and practice Indian philosophy. When I started the garden, I was practically a Buddhist—no killing animals, careful where I stepped because of the ants. That had to change a bit. I remember the first year I planted my lettuce, and when the tiny leaves started to come up I thought, "Oh, my God, it's so beautiful." The next day they were gone. I couldn't believe it and figured out it had been slugs. It was me or them, and I had to compost them.

Bees are very organized, which is something I admire them for and model myself after because the way my life is, if I don't organize myself, I can't take good care of my kids, have my garden, work on my music, or meditate. We homeschool our children so I'm with them all day while my wife goes to work; I work at night if I have a gig and in the garden in the evenings and on weekends.

There's so much here to teach my children who probably know more about bees than other people, especially my daughter who is six and very curious. She often puts on a bee suit and comes with me when I'm working with the bees, and we talk about everything. There's hardly any subject the bees don't spark—for example, the mathematics and architecture of the comb. There seems to be a whole study around just the comb and how bees make it so perfectly. After the next extraction we'll take some wax from the hive and do a candle-making project.

The other day we had a little project where we went to the garden to collect seeds. We collected thirty-six different seeds that we could name and catalogue. My daughter understands that the bees are the ones who pollinate (so plants can produce seeds) and how important pollination is to humanity's survival. Most people don't have any idea about the connection between the food on their plate and pollinators.

Right now I only have two hives. I could have more because there's plenty for them to eat, but I just don't have the time to take care of them. I had another hive that was invaded by ants because the queen was gone. I put this goopy stuff called Tanglefoot on the legs of the table that holds the hives. It keeps ants from crawling up, but apparently they found a little piece of something that enabled them to bridge it, take over the hive and steal all the honey. The comb is still fine so I'll clean the box and put the frames back on another hive. That way the bees can just fill the comb with honey and wax, and they won't have to work so much.

When it gets close to the time to do extractions, I go into the hives to scrape some of the propolis from the top of the frames. The bees make this sticky, glue-like substance from tree resin mixed with their wax, and they use it to plug every single space they can find in the hive to seal it. When they build it up from the top of the frames, the frames get so stuck to the cover that it's almost impossible to open the box. This is not what beekeepers like. In nature, bees will try to make a hive that's round. If they are inside a tree they follow the form of the trunk. In the box, we want them to build the frame straight because it's easy to get the honey out.

Sometimes I smoke them which forces them down into the safety of the hive so there's no possibility I can hurt any of them. I put some leaves along with little mesquite briquettes in the smoker, which keeps it going for quite a while. Apparently the bees think there's a fire, so they go into the hive to eat honey and prepare for flight. It also masks the smell of the beekeeper because otherwise they'd feel as if they're being attacked, and the guards would put out a pheromone to get the other bees to attack.

I put a queen excluder on and another box on top so they'll have a little more space. The excluder insures that the queen can't go into the super, so she'll be safe when I take the frames for extraction. I use the small supers because when they're full, they can weigh almost a hundred pounds. A large super would be very hard to carry. When I take each frame out for extraction I make sure there isn't even one bee on it.

Even though I only have a few hives, the extraction process takes all day. I guess for beekeepers with hundreds of hives, extracting honey is pretty much a full-time job. They extract almost every day and get tons of honey.

Once in a while a queen dies unexpectedly, and they haven't made another. Some beekeepers might just buy a queen and put her in there, but I try to integrate the queenless hive with another hive. I get a newspaper, spray it with sugar water and put it on the top of the frames. Then I put the queenless hive on top of the newspaper. They'll eat up the sugared newspaper, and the hope is that as the two hives slowly meet up, they'll be calm, mingle easily and accept each other. Sometimes it works, sometimes not. If not, you can see hundreds of dead bees on the ground in the following days because they kill each other.

My bees are either Italian or Russian; they're so mellow. Nicely, the African bees (who are aggressive) are not here yet like they are in Brazil and Latin America; in fact, there are no bees other than African there anymore. I've heard they're coming up from Latin America and are very close to the Bay Area, which they'll probably take over. When they arrive, I doubt I'll still keep bees, but until then, I'm thankful for these gentle honeybees.

The other day at the beach in Temescal Park, my daughter was playing with some friends and she came running to me saying, "I saved a bee. I saved a bee." Walking back and forth on her hand was a bee she had scooped out of the water before it drowned. It was soggy and clearly felt comfortable drying out on her hand. My daughter says she wants to save animals, and I want to nurture that passion in her.

Recently I found something I had written in a notebook and read it to her. It said, "I hope I live to see humans when they grow up to say, 'Humans should not be treated like animals.' But I hope more even to be alive when they say, 'Animals *should* be treated like humans.'"

At only six years old she got it. I hope that phrase will stay with her forever.

The Great Sunflower Project
Gretchen LeBuhn, Biology Professor
San Francisco State University,
San Francisco

I'm very interested in food security and what I call "pollinator services." I started The Great Sunflower Project several years ago when I realized we had no system for monitoring pollinator services across the United States and Canada. There were many reports that bees had declined in particular areas, and we knew about Colony Collapse Disorder. I realized that if bees were declining, we might start picking up a decrease in the number of visits that plants were getting and that we might be able to identify areas where bees were doing well or poorly, simply by looking at the rate of visitation across an area. Why not enlist the services of "citizen researchers" all over the country by having them plant a flower in their back yard and report the visitation of bees to that flower? As long as we used the same flower to measure each of these sites we could start doing some comparing. I chose Lemon Queen Sunflowers, which are the best bar in town for native bees and honeybees alike. If you're not getting visits to your Lemon Queen Sunflowers, it really says something about the bee population in your area.

> Someone could observe their sunflower every day and be my hero ....

People register on the website, plant their flowers, observe bee activity and email me the information. Observers are asked to watch their sunflower for fifteen minutes and write down each time a bee lands on it, giving us an estimate of bees per hour. That tells us something about the quality of the bee community there, and we're able to compare from yard to yard to yard, because everybody is doing exactly the same thing with the same plant. Our idea is to start identifying areas where people didn't see any bees and we can start looking at what might be the difference between that place and another where more bees are visiting the flower. Perhaps it has to do with pesticide use, pollution or landscape change. So by creating this large data base where we have lots of different places that people are doing this, we can start to pick up some of the broad scale patterns.

Someone could observe their sunflower every day and be my hero, but most people are too busy. We ask that a minimum sampling be done once at the beginning of a month and once at the end so we get a picture across the bee-flying season. We would hope that people who are noticing they're not getting bees might start thinking about how they can improve their yard, create more bee habitats or think about what's happening locally and whether they need to be paying attention to a possible early warning signal for their own community.

I've been very interested in the effects of Colony Collapse Disorder. We know that there are certain areas that have been more affected by it than others, and my hope is that we can start looking at the ratio of honeybees to native bees. If you're in an area with Colony Collapse Disorder, they're going to be mostly native bees, not honeybees. Let's say you saw five bees per hour when you had honeybees. If the next year you lost honeybees but still saw five bees per hour, that would suggest that the native bees were filling in. If it went down to being only two bees per hour that would mean that the native bees haven't been able to compensate for the loss of honeybees.

There are fewer native bees, but they can also increase in abundance fairly quickly. There's some really interesting work that a woman named Rae Winfrey's done in the Pennsylvania/New Jersey area. She's basically looked at what happens if honeybees aren't brought in to pollinate on watermelon farms and whether there's still a full seed set. The size of a watermelon depends on the number of pollen grains that a flower got, so it's a nice way to measure. If you get really good pollinator service, there's going to be a big economic benefit, so watermelon farmers have traditionally brought in a lot of honeybees. Rae was able to have some farmers who normally bring in honeybees not bring them in. She found that those farms have equally big watermelons, that the wild bee community was sufficient for performing pollinator services.

That's never going to be true, I think, for almonds or for crops in California's Central Valley, but in some areas adding honeybees to the system probably decreases the resources for native bees who are already providing sufficient pollinator services. We don't have full evidence of that and don't really know what the effect of honeybees is on native bee communities. There's evidence that in some cases the effects are detrimental. In other cases, people haven't found any effects. Honeybees provide an incredibly important service for agriculture in particular because we don't have large enough native bee communities to pollinate many of our commercial crops.

I think the reasons to have hives is that you like keeping bees and you like the honey, but in some areas it's not a good idea. San Francisco has parks with natural areas in them, and when we've sampled the native bees in those areas, we've found somewhere between sixty to a hundred species. If you compare that to Berkeley, Marin County and the Peninsula, most of those places have somewhere between two hundred to three hundred species. There's no real data to say how many species there should be in San Francisco, but there's no reason to think that it shouldn't be up around two hundred. That suggests to me that we may have lost about a hundred of our species of native bees, mostly due to habitat change. Many times in San Francisco, beekeepers want to put their hives in the wild areas of the parks, and I always suggest to the Parks and Recreation people that those are the last refuges for the native bees that live in San Francisco, and that adding honeybees into those spots probably adds pressure to these already diminished populations of native bees. In an area that has a cluster of gardens but not a park with a wild area nearby, why not have honeybees, but in other areas I would try to minimize the impact of honeybees.

The other issue that I've gotten involved in is informing the new backyard beekeepers about practicing good bee management. In the San Francisco beekeeping group, there was a new person who asked, "Why not let my bees swarm? Aren't we trying to re-up the population of honeybees?" I don't believe we should be reintroducing wild honeybee colonies to California, so it's really important that people be taught good bee husbandry by controlling swarms in order not to contribute to establishing honeybees all over the wild areas in California. That takes away from the native bees.

Here in California, there are 1,500 species of native bees, over a third of the 4,000 different species in the United States. Some are rare; some are not. Some I worry about; some I don't. That's why I think that we just want to be thoughtful about where we're keeping honeybees.

I have two hives that I keep on campus at San Francisco State. I actually do research on bumblebees, and if you're raising them in the lab, they do much better if they have fresh pollen. So I gather fresh pollen from the honeybee hives to give to the bumblebees. I have another colleague who's researching a new fly he's found that's parasitic on the honeybees. He's using my hives for that, and another person's looking at ant/bee interactions. I use my hive in my classes, plus I like getting the honey.

I've had a terrific response to people participating in The Great Sunflower Project. Getting private beekeepers to participate is wonderful because they can tell a honeybee from another bee, and I'd like to get even more data from them. One of the factors I'm really interested in is if you have a hive in your yard, does your yard actually have better pollinator service, therefore a better yield? There's a theory that says bees go three hundred yards before they start foraging, which may be an old wives' tale, but it would be really interesting and helpful to get some data from backyard beekeepers. The other thing I can look at is whether or not having a hive in your yard positively or negatively affects the probability of having native bees in your yard, something else there's no data on.

There's a great study that was done in the Central Valley where a woman looked at exactly that question: whether it was better to have both native bees and honeybees. She found that you got much better strawberries—that honeybees became three times more efficient—when there were native bees around, mostly because the native bees sort of moved them along. They actually came to the flower where the honeybee was, which made her move on quickly to the next flower, so many more got pollinated.

The Observant Beekeeper
Prodromos "Mike" Stephanos, Walnut Creek

Working with bees calms me down. I'm Type A personality, but since honeybees are definitely an even more energetic Type AA, they actually cause me to slow down. Slowing down makes me pay attention, and I begin to realize the genius in the details of what bees do.

Ever since I was a little boy I've been interested in bees. My family lived in Greece for a few years, and I spent some time on my grandfather's farm. His neighbor had bees, and I watched him work with them.

Years ago, our neighbors down the street here in Walnut Creek had a swarm in front of their house, and an older Swiss gentleman who lived a couple of blocks away came to pick them up. We started chatting about bees, and I said, "Hey, I'd really love to be a beekeeper. I'd like to learn more." I bought a hive from him for fifty dollars. It already had a super of honey, so I was instantly able to harvest the honey and extract it at his house.

One colony soon grew to two. When I learn a hobby I jump in with both feet, and because I work at home doing product development I have a schedule that allows me the time to do it. I also found a couple of mentors, Steve Gentry and Major Brunzel. Not only was I was calling my mentors between two and five times a day on different subjects pertaining to bees, I was also harassing the bees by being in their hives morning, noon and evening. Well, you're not really supposed to do that; bees have a tolerance of every

> I do what I like to call a Cincinnati Split, which is when you split a very strong colony because you know the genetics are good.

couple of days at most. I'm sure I was haranguing them and driving them nuts, but I was just so interested in what they were doing.

I went from two colonies to four rather quickly and then from four to six within two years. I held at ten for about three years—all in my backyard. Then it just started taking off and before I knew it I had sixty hives and I have been beekeeping now for twelve years. I started selling honey and realizing that this was nice little hobby. People began asking me to put bees in their yard or to teach them about bees.

One of the best places I was able to put bees was at the Rossmoor Garden Club. I had been mentoring a beekeeper there, and when he moved, he asked if I wanted to take over his two hives. I met with the club; they were delighted and said I could have as many hives as I wanted. Now I have eleven there. It's a large space adjacent to their extensive flower and vegetable garden, so the bees are a great service for pollinating. Rossmoor is a retirement community, and the residents get a kick out of knowing there are resident bees pollinating their garden. They often come by to visit me when I'm working with the hives.

Bees are under a lot of stress from the environment, so their survival rate isn't anywhere near as great as it used to be. I like to give my bees as much of a natural boost as possible. In fact, I don't like to use conventional medication anymore, but it wasn't like that when I first started.

When I began beekeeping, I basically followed the common rules of beekeeping, which was to use all the medications that most books and catalogs tell you to, to be very proactive and to prophylactically medicate, even though you don't even know if your bees have a disease. You may not have a huge mite problem, but put a miticide in there anyway. In the early days, that's what was done; now I'm firmly against that.

I believe survivor stock is what it comes down to in order to help strengthen local honeybee populations. When you catch a swarm in the wild, they're out there for a reason. They survived without medications, so that's what we call survivor stock. I no longer buy bees from breeders. I don't re-queen with commercially raised queens. I don't buy packaged bees. I only catch and repopulate with swarms. I'm fortunate to catch a lot of swarms here because I'm well-known in the area so people call me for swarm removal. Among those who call me are exterminators because they know I keep the bees alive. Not only do I supply myself with bees, I supply kids at the 4-H and other members of our bee club with survivor stock swarms.

We don't really know where those swarms are coming from, but the majority come from holes in trees, walls of houses or upside-down flower pots etc. If they're from another beekeeper's hive who may medicate, you just don't know. In some cases one may find a marked queen which indicates it is from a managed hive. I prefer to mark my queens because then I know if the queen has been superseded (killed and/or replaced) if I find an unmarked queen in my hive. This is a clear indication that my old queen has been naturally replaced.

I do what I like to call a Cincinnati Split, which is when you split a very strong colony. Say, after a year or two, I find that one of my colonies is very, very strong and productive, then I know it has great genetics. In fact, they're so strong, they probably will swarm. So I like to preempt that swarm and split the hive, hopefully eliminating the swarming instinct for the year.

I take some comb with eggs out, find and isolate the queen in the original hive, and create two hives. I take half of the colony with fresh eggs that the queen has just laid, some larvae, some capped brood and some of the house bees, and I move them to another box.

Soon a virgin queen will be born, fly and mate with multiple drones. We don't know the genetics of those partners, but at least we know the genetic qualities of the new queen. We know then that the new colony should have some quality traits that we have perpetuated from the queen's genetic line. Not only will we have quality strengths, we'll have qualities of good hygiene—cleaning the hive, taking care of the mites and many other issues.

In nature, bees like plenty of space and ventilation; they control the amount of ventilation by filling in little cracks in the hive with propolis. To provide the bees with additional ventilation in the heat of summer, I use screened bottom boards (which is also a useful pest management device). I like propping hive tops, allowing much more ventilation through the hive. I don't want to give them too much space, but I want to give them enough, so I always try to run what's called "two-deep hive bodies"—two lower brood boxes—which give the queen plenty of space to lay eggs and for the worker bees to store adequate pollen and honey. I provide additional space for honey during the nectar flow by adding medium suppers as needed.

I've been very fortunate to be mentored by quite a few veteran beekeepers, whom I greatly respect. I've collected their knowledge as much as possible and applied it to what's best for the bees and also to what's convenient for my style of beekeeping. For example, many veteran beekeepers do not use queen excluders in the hive; instead, they allow the queen to move up into the fresh comb of the honey supers. When the nectar flow hits full swing, the worker bees start to put honey up above the brood. This forces the queen slowly down into the lower boxes.

I use queen excluders just because it makes my life a little easier; I do not have to worry about the queen being in the honey super when I harvest. That's me being selfish and saying, "No, you can't go up there, queen, but you can let your worker bees put honey up there for me."

Through the years I've seen how strong hives can fight off ants; if a hive is unable to deal with ants, its an indication it is weak. I like to give the bees a little boost by going out to gather eucalyptus leaves which ants don't like, dragging them back in a big burlap bag, and sprinkling them around the hive. This is one of many natural ways to fight pests that impact the bees

In the early days when I only had a few hives I used to paint designs like waves, dots and checkerboards on their front above the entrance of the hive. When several beehives are close together, there's an element of drift (wind pushing bees). If it's a windy day, some bees will drift from one hive to the other by accident. The neighboring hive will accept the random few, but not very many. Bees can recognize shape and tonality, so I painted individual designs on each hive so the bees could recognize and thus help them target their hive more accurately. This is called a "bee address."

There are basically two types of beekeepers. There's the beekeeper and the keeper of bees. A beekeeper is somebody who understands bees, who really gets involved with them. It comes very naturally and intuitively. People who have a technical sense seem to pick up an understanding of bees much more readily than those who are less technical.

Then there's the keeper of bees. I've mentored a couple of people who are very sweet, very kind and extremely interested in bees, but after two or three years, they just don't grasp what's going on in the hive. They can read everything under the sun, and yet it just doesn't connect for them. For those people, just having bees in their life is very fulfilling. They have a hive in the garden and allow the bees to go about life on their own, never getting involved in the technical aspects of beekeeping.

Over the years I've been beekeeping, my style has evolved towards "a less is more" attitude. Bees have been around for a lot longer than we have, so we have to realize that they know what they're doing. I no longer always have to be in the brood boxes. I don't always have to find the queen. I don't have to medicate. I prefer to observe them and let them tell me what's going on. I can know exactly what their health is, what the condition of the hive is, how they're feeling, etc., just by observing from outside the hive. Bees give lots of clues, and a good beekeeper has to be aware of those clues. That comes in time and from patient observation.

This past summer I was away for three months. The few times I came back, I walked around the hives and looked at all my bees, but I didn't go into the hives. I didn't have to suit up; I just looked at them. I could tell how they were faring by how they were flying, what the entrance looked like, the volume of the bees. I lifted a corner of the hive to feel weight of the hive to see if they were putting away honey. You can smell if a hive is sick. If they have foul brood it smells like dirty socks. If they have nosema—bee dysentery—it looks like tobacco spit on the front of the hive. By the way they're acting on the front of the stoop, you can tell if they have major mites issue (for example if there are bees not fully developed). You can tell if you have chalk brood if in the early morning there are mummified bees on the front stoop of the hive.

Honey not only has an amazing taste but there's no doubt in my mind that it also has beneficial health qualities, even curative powers. On popular television talk shows, one can hear the talk about taking honey from the pantry to the medicine cabinet. I think this is true—and not just because I'm a beekeeper. I think there are other things that we overlook and take for granted in nature that can cure many of our ailments. There's a pendulum that swings, and I think we've gone from the natural perspective to a heavy pharmaceutical. Our bodies are getting so tired of that stuff that we need to look back to the natural and find a balance.

A Place of Healing
The Melissa Garden Honeybee Sanctuary
Barbara & Jacques Schlumberger, Healdsburg

Here at the Melissa Garden the buzzing of bees is not only audible but practically tangible, and flowers—vehicles of life for pollinators—explode from every inch. The air is filled with the movement of many beings feeding on the brilliant bounty.

My husband and I started the Melissa Garden at our home in Healdsburg, California in 2007. Located on top of a ridge at the western edge of the Russian River Valley, the Melissa Garden is a honeybee, native pollinator and habitat garden sanctuary. Our goal is to provide honeybees, native bees (of which there are 1700 species in California) and other pollinators with an almost year-round source of floral resources—all free from pesticides. We chose the name "Melissa" not only because it is the Greek word for honeybee but is also the scientific name for Lemon Balm, an herbaceous plant that is a favorite of honeybees and one of the top plants that supports their health.

> The exuberance of flowers and explosive colors have attracted many people as well as pollinators. The Melissa Garden has become a garden of life to feed all visitors....

Four gardens planted with many exuberant flowers for nectar and pollen forage are situated in the center of our pristine forty-acre ranch, lush with native vegetation. There's an existing orchard of twenty trees and many bee-friendly plants around our house. Studies have found that both honeybees and native bees benefit from feeding on a variety of flowers, so season-long the garden is kept filled with an abundance of annuals, perennials and shrubs that offer attractive pollen and nectar to insect visitors. There is a mixture of plants native to California, many Mediterranean plants, and others that are appropriate for the site and climate. Quantity of nectar and quality of pollen, timed throughout the year to support the seasonal needs of the hive, are the key guidelines in our plant selection. We didn't want plants that honeybees simply visit; we wanted to select plants that honeybees clearly love and are the most nourishing to strengthen them and help them fight disease. Over time, we've discovered that Phacelia, Borage, Echium, Melissa, Goldenrod and Cilantro are among the top plants that support honeybees with nectar and pollen throughout the season. Having good sources of resin nearby is also important because honeybees make propolis, known for it's ability to inhibit bacterial growth and insure the hygiene of the hive.

Terroir is an important concept in regard to honeybee forage. The locale is captured in the nectar and pollen and ultimately in the honey. Plants express themselves totally based on where they are planted, the fertility of the ground, and the gardening methods used. Honeybees, from the human perspective, are mercurial. While they might go for pollen from crocuses in one garden in the early spring, they may completely ignore them in another garden if they find botanicals they like better. They are always attuned to finding the best pollen and nectar sources available.

The exuberance of flowers and explosive colors have attracted many people as well as pollinators. The Melissa Garden has become a garden of life to feed all visitors, and many people come to visit: bee-tenders, school classes, University of California Master Gardeners, garden clubs, professional gardeners, scientists, and the general public who are concerned about the plight of honeybees and biodiversity and want to learn about gardens that support them. The garden's vibrant colors, naturalistic plant compositions, and intense buzzing life have created deep connections with people, and many leave inspired to plant their own pollinator or habitat gardens, fulfilling exactly the main goal of our project.

Here at the Melissa Garden, we live with the bees under a new paradigm, which is actually a very ancient way of seeing honeybees. We consider ourselves bee-stewards and approach the phenomena of the bees on the premise that a colony constitutes one single being. Our focus is shifted towards the study of the colonies' life forces, and our interaction with them is centered around their natural needs on all levels. We use no allopathic treatments, instead providing them the forage they need to strengthen their immune system so they can fight disease and the Varroa mite naturally. Particularly important is cilantro, which is like an antibiotic for honeybees.

Since we're situated on forty acres with no close neighbors, we allow our bees to swarm. If we can catch the swarms we'll put them in hives, but if we don't catch them, they find a tree or a nest somewhere. We're trying to do that more and more to allow them to survive out in the wild.

We use innovative hives that allow comb building that is much more natural and are not invasive to check. All provide an environment for bees that is closer to their natural gestalt, giving them the space to build comb with greater depth than regular beehives.

Occasionally we go into a hive to be sure it's not honey-bound—that there's enough room for the bees to put their honey and for the queen to lay 2,000 eggs a day. I don't wear protection anymore. I simply go in gently and slowly, which does not disturb the bees. With our hives, a wax cloth lies gently on the top so it's possible to roll it back slightly to look unobtrusively at a small part of the hive and then roll it back again quietly.

We harvest only truly surplus honey, and because of this, all our hives have plenty to winter-over on their own food. If we take honey, which we rarely do, we cut the comb out and squeeze it the way they used to in the old days. We let it drip out in the warm sun, and then we melt the wax and make candles. The bees make more comb, which is what they've been doing for two hundred million years.

By becoming "bee-stewards" and understanding the bees' natural needs and lifecycles, we benefit the world by seeing bees as part of our human culture and well-being, realizing how they can enrich our lives on many levels. The Melissa Garden is committed to allowing honeybees to live in a natural way. That, if anything, is what will save them.

THE BEEKEEPERS

A Different Kind of Beekeeper
Michael Thiele, Gaia Bees, Sebastopol

There are so many beautiful things about honeybees and many reasons why they are in our lives. They fascinate us and can even touch our hearts. That's the quality I think every beekeeper knows. Many say they can forget the sorrows of their lives and relax into some kind of happiness without words when they go to the bees.

I came from Germany to California for a retreat after my wife died of cancer. Death brings so many things to an end; I didn't know what would come next, but my life opened up again in a way I would never have imagined. The retreat was at a Benedictine monastery in Big Sur, which I was attracted to because of Brother David Steindl-Rast. Although he's a Catholic monk, he practices Zen because he is very engaged in interfaith dialogue.

He introduced me to the San Francisco Zen Center and I started practicing Zen at Green Gulch in Marin County. There I met my second wife, we raised our two children, and I entered the world of honeybees. We lived there for almost ten years until we moved five years ago to Sebastopol.

> Bees are an indicator species, reflecting the health of our environment as well as the interdependence and interconnectedness of all life on earth.

One of my family members in Germany kept bees, so I had been exposed to them from an early age. One winter while I was living at Green Gulch, I started having dreams about bees, and that spring, when swarms kept coming, I thought, *Well, I guess it's time for me to start beekeeping.*

A friend lent me an empty hive, which I put behind my house. One day I was working in the garden across the pond and heard people calling me because there was a huge swarm circling our tiny house, trying to get into the hive. It wasn't open enough for them to get in, but, of course, they smelled it. So I opened it a little more and it was like the genie going into the bottle; they all moved in, and I became a beekeeper.

I didn't know much about bees, but I had a real feeling for them, and out of that emotional relating many, many things began unfolding. I felt drawn to their own wisdom and allowed them to express that wisdom in their instinctual, natural way. I began to truly understand that the single bee is only one individual part of the bigger entity of the entire beehive. This can serve as a beautiful metaphor or mirror for our own existence: That we humans are just one individual part of a bigger entity—the earth's ecosystem and the entire universe.

Bees are an indicator species, reflecting the health of our environment as well as the interdependency and interconnectedness of all life on earth. Traditional beekeeping understood and acknowledged the natural life forces of the bees, but modern beekeeping practices have lost this ancient knowledge, and this loss has taken its toll on the bees. I believe that we need to know who the bees are; only then can we serve them through our actions and do the best we can to support them in these times. In order to help us help the honeybees, we need to open our senses to understand them and shift paradigms.

It's very tricky, however, because the main tool we have is language, and language is always seated in a certain paradigm. For example, the way we currently describe bees within that paradigm is by distinguishing between three elements, which we call the queen, the worker bee, and the drone. I began thinking, does that language reflect the nature of those elements or does it rather reflect our intentions and our world view? The problem is that language can limit our senses and our understanding, which in turn can prevent us from true understanding.

Take the queen. Is the queen truly a queen in the human sense of one being ruling or having control over others? Well, when we look at it, we find that the queen is so interwoven within the entity of the whole hive, so intertwined that she is actually not at all in charge. She may be the carrier of the very important eggs to create more bees—like a certain soul element—and the particular scent of that one colony, but it is the female worker bees who make the two different sized cells in which she puts the eggs. The small cells are for so-called worker bees; the larger cells are for so-called drones. So who decides which size cell to build, when there are over a hundred bees on average being part of the construction of one single cell? The queen will come and lay an egg. She is actually quite choiceless, because if she finds a small cell, she has no choice but to lay a fertilized egg, which will be a female bee; in a larger cell, she will lay an unfertilized egg which will be a male bee.

Now take the worker bee. I find that label very challenging. It's unfortunate, because it doesn't serve our understanding. Isn't it a shame that we reduce that little creature to something which works, meaning produces, meaning produces honey for *us*? There's so much more to her. They're the females, but they're doing all the physical work. They carry the stinger and have venom, so they have this aggressive potential, and yet they redefine that potential through the fact that if they use it, they will sacrifice their own life because they will die. So the use of their stinger is absolutely defensive, and I find it so beautiful to look at how the energy is used within the bee, how it's attached to that condition of sacrifice. Suppose we humans knew if we used our aggression offensively we'd die. Aggression, traditionally a typical male attribute, is here in the female energy, used *only* to defend the wholeness of the colony. Then, of course, we have this beautiful nursing of the offspring within the nature of the females; those same bees are caring—it's all about service, caring for the offspring, protecting the hive and being an essential element for the fertility of the earth.

Then we come to the drones. The negative connotation of the word is that the drone is a plump, useless nuisance. I discovered that the word drone also describes the deep humming sound they make when flying. But the first connotation is the one we use to say they are useless, not only because they are not out foraging for nectar, but also because inside the hive they're being fed honey. They're eating "my" honey. Once we call them "drones," our mind may close. We are not curious to really find out what they really are or what they really do. What important roles do they play?

The drones don't have a stinger. They are very round, usually a more feminine characteristic. When you look at their head it consists almost completely of those two large eyes. Drones grow up in the cells that are all the way around the brood nest, which is in the center and contain the females. It's almost as if there's some shielding, some protection happening, or maybe it's a warming quality.

The really interesting thing about those drones is they leave the hive mostly in the early afternoon, especially in the springtime, and go to the so-called drone congregations where they wait for the queen to come and then chase her to mate with her. Once they've mated with the queen, they die. They did what they needed to do; it's part of their life, and then they die.

Those drone congregations are bees from many different hives. I feel like part of their life is about communicating and networking, because drones can go back to their own hive, but also they can go to other colonies or "families." Each family has its own scent. The world of bees is so much about scent. If a foreign female bee arrives at the entrance of a hive, they won't let her in, but drones can go in.

So just imagine, those drones starting out in one hive and perhaps ending up in different hives many, many miles away. There's this networking quality about those drones, and I believe we still don't know all the ways, all of the functions, and all of the features they serve.

We say the drones are "pushed out of hive" at the end of the summer after the queen has been mated and the remaining ones are no longer needed. It sounds brutal. Again, language. Another way of describing what's happening is that that male energy knows that it doesn't have to be incarnated in the winter months. So it will let go of its embodiment. It will let go of its physical form, retreat and perish, only to come back in the spring when it's time to play its role again. In fact, male energy is giving its life at this critical time for the winter survival of the colony. The drones sacrifice themselves because it's critical for the colony to have enough food throughout the winter.

The life span of the summer female bee is maybe seven weeks, and her work is not for herself, but for all those generations down the line. Everything in the colony is communal; everything is shared. No bee has her own little honey cell or her own little pollen cell or her own children; she is completely dedicated to give and to serve the community. A bee's entire life is dedicated to the wholeness. I find that very inspirational on a heart level. Most religions are centered on love and service. Maybe that goes too far, but somehow, don't we all yearn for that sense of being able to happily give and serve and recognize how deeply we're all connected and dependent on each other, instead of just our own little separate individual beings? The hive has a palpable quality, which has to do with service. It's serving through pollination. It's huge to the planet and us humans, too.

It's so rich. We see 50,000 bees in a hive, and yet there's a feeling of oneness. When you go back to what defines an organism, one essential element is that there's a membrane, something which separates what is called the inner environment and the outer environment—just like our skin—and within, we can control warmth, the flow of energy, and many more things. When you apply that definition to a bee colony, you find that there is an invisible membrane that makes it into a oneness, a super organism—that which goes beyond the individual organism. I like to call it "Bien." Thousands of bees are integrated into a higher-order entity, whose ability far transcends that of the individual bee. Their communication and networking capacities, non-hierarchical decision processes, and an understanding of service to the greater web of life are pointing to a higher level of development and awareness. As such, the bees are a vital part of human culture and an inspiration to the soul.

I want to say something about comb because it is fascinating and mind-boggling. I am passionate about it because beekeepers generally ignore it, and it's so integral to the colony. Comb is made from wax that comes out of the bees' bodies. Bees hang from each other, the gravity always pulling on them, and therefore, comb is built with gravity. They know exactly where's up and where's down. That's why comb always goes straight down, because the wax is created by those hanging bees.

Apparently, (according to biologist Juergen Tautz) they start building out round cells. Through body warmth, they heat them up to 107.6° F, at which point the properties of wax change as the fluid properties become more dominant. Suddenly those rounded cells literally pop into place and join each other. Imagine two completely round soap bubbles floating in the air, but when they meet, their common wall becomes completely straight. This has to do with properties of fluidity and surface tension. When the bees are in the middle of creating comb, they heat the wax to its critical threshold for becoming more fluid, round meets with round creating a straight edge and that's when those hexagonal cells form.

THE BEEKEEPERS

The whole comb—especially the rims of each cell—are coated with a fine film of propolis, which has antifungal, antibacterial properties. Bees keep the hive at around 98.6° F (the temperature of warm-blooded animals), whether it is freezing outside or stiflingly hot. At this temperature the wax can resonate with vibrations from the bees. The beauty is that during the waggle dance, they not only do this figure eight form, but as they dance, they hold on to the rims of the cells and vibrate at a certain frequency (250 hertz per second). Warm comb produces the best resonance at 250 hertz, so it's part of their communication system and an example of how comb is really an integral part of that being.

Beeswax has a certain scent, and it changes over time. The life of bees inside the hive is happening in darkness and as they walk across the comb, their antennae sense the wax. They know where they are, what kind of wax it is, how old it is, and the whole history of that hive.

Because of all this, I never use a Langstroth hive anymore. Sometimes people feel offended by this, and I feel sorry that they do, but I don't believe in them. When you really look closely, a Langstroth hive is designed for the convenience of the beekeeper, but not for the benefit of the honeybee.

In a natural hive, comb grows downward. Langstroth frames are horizontal and shallow. You have a frame, then free space, then a frame, etc. so you have interrupted comb, not a unified structure. The way Langstroths are added on to is on top. It's very challenging for bees to add to empty space above, because they then need to generate a critical mass of bees to make that leap up and build comb downward.

When you put foundation in a Langstroth hive, the myth is that you save lots of honey, which would have been used to create that wax. In modern beekeeping with plastic foundations, there is only one cell size in the hive—the smaller one, so through that practice of using foundations, we actually remove a very important element of that animal.

That's huge. We're taking away that male element. Only a very few drone cells may be built in small niches of the hive.

With plastic foundation, vibration doesn't work anymore. That right there already interferes with their communication system. We haven't even talked about the components of the foundations and how polystyrene with the benzene is carcinogenic. Eggs are laid in partial plastic. What are the logical implications of that? Plastic is an implant; we should not call it foundation. It's an implant, and it should be regulated according to implants, but that's not done.

I mainly use the Golden Hive, which was designed to provide an environment that's sustainable to the energy and life force of the colony but also enables us to be apiculturists. The dimensions of the one-room-hive are set according to the "Golden Mean," or "divine proportion"—a universal principle within all forming forces in nature also found in art, architecture and ancient philosophy. The entire colony lives in one room with twenty tall frames that allow for the natural downward flow of comb and the development of a large brood nest, which is a protected space. The top bar of each frame is beveled and looks like a boat keel. It's a rounded shape that ends up in a very thin edge, a beautiful surface for them to start building comb, and they naturally go there. Honey can be received from the sides of the hive, and we do not put supers on. A wax cloth lays on top of the frames and protects the inner climate of the "Bien". A side window enables the beekeeper to receive information about the hive without having to open it too often. Bees are very calm in this kind of hive and easy to work with.

So for us apiculturists to be able to get information about honeybees' well-being without necessarily having to open the hives too much, Golden Hives provide features for a less invasive way of being with them. When you open a hive, in some ways, you're entering the interior of that being. I think about how intimately bees are connected with their comb, so by having that wax blanket in place and peeling it back slowly, it protects them from a sudden draft and from losing that integrity right away. It's a gentle, respectful way of entering the hive, and the benefit for the apiculturist is that the bees are so much calmer. When you open a Langstroth hive, you create a draft, and all the warmth, the scent, and the humidity is disrupted. Then you have to rip the frames apart just to look into the box.

I do get honey from the hives, but certainly not as much as from Langstroth hives. That's definitely a difference, but then you have to ask, what really is the price to the bees?

With a Golden Hive, you take the honey out by lifting one of the frames. The bees have built the comb from top to bottom. It's so beautiful. Since it's long, there are no extractors for that size, so you either keep it as comb honey, or you crush it. I crush it because it enriches the honey, but even more importantly, I believe it's very, very important for bees to rebuild comb. There are all those worrisome studies about how pesticide traces are building up in comb. Nowadays even conventional science is suggesting letting them build new comb, otherwise you'll end up having contaminated comb in the nursery and the baby bees will grow up in that toxic environment. It's another paradigm shift. In the olden days, people were proud of having these black comb frames — ten, twenty years old — and today some beekeepers feel the same way, but it's not working any more. We are living in a different world.

It's extremely rare that I would use a bee suit. Sometimes some of those tools are necessary, and it's definitely good to go with one's comfort level because the bees sense our anxiety, but the tricky part is when we suit up, we don't have to pay attention to them anymore. We can do whatever we want, and all that armor will prevent us from understanding who honeybees are on a deeper level. We've already set up not only a physical barrier but a mind barrier. So we march in and take them apart and do all of those things, and the sad part is that we truly lose. We lose those beautiful ways—slow and gentle—of being with that creature. We lose the possibility of empathy. We lose the opportunity to touch the pulse of life, to touch the pulse of our own heart.

Honeybees let a gentle beekeeper go in peacefully; they're opening themselves in a way. You read signs. You approach them slowly; you look at the entrance; you listen—how do they sound? Are there a lot of guard bees? Are they nervous? You get to know them in a different way. You open up all of your senses, and then you know when you have to smoke and when you don't. I remember one hive we didn't smoke. We opened the wax blanket a little bit, and they seemed nervous. We closed the blanket, and maybe a minute later, we started again, and they were calmer. One thing you can do is smoke yourself, especially your hands, and then put the smoker away and go to the bees instead of smoking *them*. It will cover any kind of funny scent on yourself.

I am the co-founder of the Melissa Garden where I set up the bee program and teach most of the bee classes. I have my own hives at home. I sell Golden Hives and other alternative hives and help people set up their apiaries. Some people want me not only to set them up but also to tend them. If someone wants a Langstroth hive, then they have to find someone else.

Honeybees touch me on my heart level in a way I want to say only whales can. I've seen whales, and just the sheer sight of them made me cry. I now feel like that with bees, but it's taken time to let the restrictive language disappear, to stretch my range of perception and to open up. A dualistic world view is so ingrained in us. There's you, and there's me. There's a beehive filled with honeybees that will pollinate my garden and give me honey. Maybe I'm trying to say we have to shift back and dedicate our life more to find the unity, what really connects us. I'm saying anybody can learn to feel that with honeybees. Could that connection become a window to a different kind of understanding of life and the world as we know it? Could it be a doorway to another aspect of consciousness?

6
CONCENTRATED GOODNESS

... whatever we have got has been by infinite labor, and search, and ranging through every corner of nature; the difference is that instead of dirt and poison, we have rather chosen to fill our hives with honey and wax, thus furnishing mankind with the two noblest of things, which are sweetness and light.

--Jonathan Swift

CONCENTRATED GOODNESS

Honey, the first sweetener used by humans, is a totally benign, sustainable food. It starts as water that gathers minerals from the earth as it is drawn up into the flower, is made into nectar within the flower, sucked out by the bee who takes it back to the hive where enzymes are added, and it is reduced it to its essence. Its creation hurts nothing and nobody.

Honey is eternal. Totally pure and free of bacteria, it needs no pasteurization and if kept sealed, never spoils. Over two hundred years ago archaeologists found a container of 3,000-year-old honey in an Egyptian tomb, and it was still edible. Honey has an endless shelf life not only in a tomb but in the pantry.

It's not surprising that this pure food has enormous health benefits and even curative powers. In addition to honey, pollen, royal jelly, venom, wax and propolis all have value to humans, some of it only beginning to be understood.

A Flavor of Place

Honey, like wine, has a "flavor of place," a provenance, a terroir. It is influenced by the soil and climate of the region and varies according to what nectars bees have drunk. It may take its taste from a single type of flower if that is what is primarily available or from a combination of several nectars in the area. Honeys vary in color depending on their source and mineral content—practically clear to shades of gold to amber to dark brown to everything in between. Flavors range from mild to strong, delicate to pungent.

Varietal or monofloral honey comes from a single type of flower like apple blossom, orange blossom, or lavender. Besides the actual flavor of the honey, you can taste the flavor that comes from the flower. A blended honey is a mixture from different sources and has a less distinct flavor. "Wildflower" is often used to describe honey from undefined flower sources.

Eucalyptus honey varies in color and flavor but generally has a slightly medicinal or pepperminty taste. Besides being used as a sweetener, some say it settles the nerves and soothes the mucous membranes. Orange blossom honey is light in color with a mild citrus taste and a fresh, clean scent. Lime blossom honey has a clear, intense, flavor; apple blossom honey has a sweet, floral essence. Acacia honey is clear with a light, delicate, almost vanilla flavor, whereas avocado honey is dark with a rich, buttery taste. Some say lavender honey has anti-inflammatory properties for the respiratory tract. Pale, almost white, it has a mild flavor but unmistakably lavender. Thyme honey is aromatic and considered a delicacy. Sage is full-bodied but has a mild flavor; sunflower is delicate, and manzanita is earthy and spicy.

CONCENTRATED GOODNESS

Honey Extraction

Honeybees cap the cells that contain honey with wax, creating a tidy storage cell. In a Langstroth hive, the first step in extracting honey, therefore, is to remove the caps, which is usually done by a hot knife. The frames are suspended in a big metal tub which spins the honey to the sides by centrifugal force. Honey drips down the sides to the bottom and must be passed through a screen to separate it from little pieces of wax or the occasional bee leg.

But how is it assured that only honey is extracted—not brood innocently incubating in their cells? In a feral hive the queen lays eggs in the center of the hive to keep the brood warm. Around the brood-laying area are cells filled with pollen, which is easily accessible for nurse bees to feed the emerging young. Larger drone cells are created on the periphery, and honey is usually kept in the upper part of the hive. Using the feral hive as a model, in a man-made frame hive the center frames contain the queen and brood where it's darkest, warmest and most protected. When a super is added, the bees will store their honey in that upper box. Often the beekeeper adds a "queen excluder" on top of the lower box which has openings that only the small worker bees can fit through, assuring that the larger queen will stay below. The beekeeper removes the frames from the super that contain only honey and no possibility of the queen or developing larvae.

Healthy Honey

Honey contains a wide variety of vitamins, minerals, amino acids, carbohydrates, antioxidants and water. When the bees process the nectar by adding enzymes, complex sugars are broken down into simpler ones, making honey easily digestible and soothing to the human digestive tract. Unlike refined sugar, which careens into the bloodstream and then causes a crash, sugars in honey enter the blood stream at different rates: glucose is absorbed quickly, providing an immediate energy boost followed by fructose, which is absorbed more slowly, giving sustained energy.

Honey can accelerate the healing of an open wound. Because of its osmotic properties—its ability to extract and absorb water—honey applied to a wound leaves little water on which infection-causing bacteria survive. Because of the enzymes in honey, hydrogen peroxide is produced, which actually kills bacteria. Honey stimulates the growth of tissue and reduces scarring. Its anti-inflammatory properties can help reduce pain and improve circulation, which also speeds up the healing process. On ancient, bloody battlefields, honey was used to dress wounds, and during World War I, soldiers carried a mixture of honey and cod liver oil, which they applied to even the most severe injuries.

As a natural antiseptic, honey is often used as a topical treatment for burns, soothing and helping prevent scarring. It has been used to store skin grafts for up to twelve weeks. As an anti-microbial agent, it deters the growth of certain types of bacteria, yeast and molds. In certain cases where leg or foot ulcers or abscesses have not responded to traditional treatment using antibiotics and antiseptics, honey has been used to heal these wounds.

The ancients used honey on their skin and it's still a major ingredient in today's skin care products. Combined with coconut oil, it makes a wonderful hydrating mask, giving nourishment and moisture to the skin. Because of its antibacterial properties, it works well as a body scrub that cleanses and leaves the body bacteria free.

Many people believe eating small amounts of local honey can help with allergies.

Bee Pollen

Bee pollen, one of the richest, purest and most complete natural foods, seems almost too good to be true. In fact, some call it a miracle food. Honeybees pack it into the comb to feed their young as a protein source. It can be extracted from the frames of modern hives but involves a painstaking method.

When ingested by humans, bee pollen helps oxygen reach the brain cells and strengthens capillary walls. It cleans the blood and can regulate the intestines. It contains protein, all 22 known amino acids, enzymes, vitamins A, the Bs, C, D, E, K and the many minerals including calcium, phosphorus, potassium, iron, manganese, zinc, titanium and copper. It has no cholesterol. Although it contains fats, it is naturally low in calories. Athletes often use it to increase their strength and endurance.

Royal Jelly

Royal Jelly is the powerful substance fed to all larvae in the colony for the first few days of their lives. It is made of pollen and honey, which nurse bees chew up and mix with a chemical they secrete. It is the substance that turns an ordinary bee into the queen merely by feeding the chosen larvae *only* royal jelly not only during her first few days but for the rest of her life.

Royal jelly, rich in protein and B vitamins, also contains an antibiotic substance. So far, scientists have been unable to break it into all its specific components and it cannot be synthesized. It has been claimed as a cognitive enhancer, able to stimulate neural cells in the brain. Preliminary research shows it may have some cholesterol-lowering effects, along with anti-cancer and anti-inflammatory properties.

Royal jelly has been used by both men and women for rejuvenation, and some claim it is a sexual stimulant. There is continuing research about its use in slowing aging, helping arthritis, vascular disease, ulcers, skin problems and nervous conditions.

Bee Venom

Being stung by bees for therapeutic purposes is nothing new. The Chinese first did acupuncture with bee stingers; the ancient Egyptians and Romans used it to treat various ailments, and in Greece, Hippocrates used bee venom over 2,400 years ago to treat arthritis and rheumatism. Apitherapy is much more common in Eastern Europe, Asia and South America than the United States. The use of bee venom has not been thoroughly tested, but there are suggestions that it can be effective in the treatment of not only arthritis and rheumatism but also high blood pressure, high cholesterol, multiple sclerosis, lupus, scleroderma and other autoimmune diseases.

Beeswax

Bees secrete little flakes of wax from their abdomen and mix it with saliva to build their comb. Humans use it for candles, furniture polish and in art materials. It is also a component in cosmetics and a binder in drugs.

A paraffin candle doesn't "hold a candle" to one made of beeswax. A beeswax candle burns brighter, its flame surrounded by a lovely halo and smells like honey as it burns. It doesn't drip on your linen tablecloth or give off smoke. Because of its high melting point, it burns thirty percent longer than paraffin, and as it burns it purifies the air by creating negative ions which rid the air of toxins and allergens. Beeswax comes from a renewable source, whereas paraffin is derived from crude oil.

Propolis

The inside of a beehive is one of the most sterile environments possible. Bees collect sticky resin from tree bark and combine it with pollen, nectar and wax to make propolis, which has potent anti-microbial and anti-fungal properties. They plug holes and cracks in the hive with propolis and also apply a thin coating over the cells, which prevents harmful bacteria from entering the hive. At the entrance to their hive they create a small tunnel of the substance, and as they squeeze through the tunnel, harmful microbes picked up in the field are scraped off.

Naturopaths use propolis for superficial burns, as an anti-inflammatory and to combat viruses. Recent studies have looked into propolis as an agent to combat tumor growth. It is used as the base for wood varnish and it is said that the luthier Antonio Stradivari used it in the crafting of his violins.

7
GARDEN NOTES: WE NEED ALL THE POLLINATORS WE CAN GET

A garden can serve a bigger purpose
than simply prettying a yard.
   -Gordon Frankie

WE NEED ALL THE POLLINATORS WE CAN GET

The garden...sanctuary and buffer from the civilized world. Today more critical than ever, the garden can also be a nourishing stopover for honeybees and other pollinators when filled with plants they like and need. As essential to a garden as dirt, water and sunlight, pollinators make our gardens prolific and sustainable. By supporting them, we make a personal, immediate and positive difference in the current crisis of dwindling forage, and the effect ripples out to the entire ecosystem. Whether you have a flower garden, an edible garden, orchard or combination; whether your taste leans toward Zen or lush Victorian; whether you're a zealous digger or a putterer, make your garden an oasis for pollinators. Encourage your neighbors to make their yards pollinator-friendly, since an entire corridor of abundant forage is better than isolated patches. We need all the pollinators we can get!

Above all, an organic garden is crucial to the health of pollinators who unfortunately are exposed to insecticides, pesticides and herbicides elsewhere.

A variety of colors and shapes attracts honeybees, native bees and other pollinators. Most nurseries in the Bay

Area now label their plants to indicate which pollinators they are best suited for. Honeybees are attracted to bright colors, mainly yellow, blue and purple; to them, red appears dull. They love sweet fragrances and prefer cup-shaped flowers with marks like a landing platform. Some of these marks are visible to the human eye, but more often, "honey guides" on flowers can be seen only by honeybees.

Native bees prefer native plants and are drawn to blue, yellow, white, purple and pink rather than orange or red. Native California plants have adapted to this climate, making them self-reliant and requiring less water than many non-native plants. Many of the exotics that have found their way to California and thrive here, however, have almost become naturalized and provide excellent nectar and pollen sources, so a combination of native and exotic plants can work well.

Hummingbirds, entertaining with their antics as they hover, fly upside down or even backwards, are excellent pollinators. They have good eyes but a poor sense of smell, are attracted to brightly colored flowers (especially red and orange) and do not like flowers with strong scents. The flowers dust the little bird's body with pollen as it hovers — wings beating up to 78 times a second — and sips. Ever-moving, the hummingbird spends only three or four seconds at a flower, then flutters on, and as it dips into the next flower for nectar, pollen rubs off. Be aware of flowers like bougainvillea, which have nectarless blossoms and only trick hummingbirds into wasting their precious energy.

Perhaps because of their nocturnal nature and strange looks, bats are difficult for people to warm up to. Knowing that a mother bat gives birth to her young and breast feeds them, not to mention that a single bat can eat 600 mosquitoes

WE NEED ALL THE POLLINATORS WE CAN GET

in only one hour, hopefully softens our perception of them since they are important pollinators. Bats evolved to be drawn to white or light-colored, musty smelling flowers, which open at night. The flowers must be large and sturdy enough to accommodate the bat's head.

Butterflies can see red but don't have much of a sense of smell, so the flowers they pollinate are brightly-colored, but unscented. Butterflies like a leisurely pace, perching when they feed, so often the flowers they like grow in clusters to provide a broad landing field. The butterfly meanders around the cluster, probing the flower for nectar with its long tongue, picking up pollen in the process. They are daytime feeders, whereas moths feed at night, so flowers seeking the moth's attention are white or light-colored and visible in the dark. Since moths have a good sense of smell, the flowers have a strong scent. Because the moth doesn't linger on the flower, the petals are bent back or flat to give her easy access as she moves quickly from flower to flower.

Just one plant, or even several, will not draw either honeybees or solitary bees. Planting a drift about four feet square of the same flower is a more powerful attractor for all bees. Plant for continuous bloom. A succession of blooms not only offers an uninterrupted flow of beauty, but also provides a continuous source of pollen and nectar throughout the year. We are fortunate in the Bay Area that there is very little down-time as far as plants go. With good planning, as one plant dies, another bursts into life. Leave no gaps, and the pollinators will keep coming.

If possible, leave some less manicured space. Solitary native bees nest in the ground or in trees and love sun and dry places. Leave some areas with loose dirt and an occasional dead tree branch. You can also provide places for wild bees to nest by drilling holes about five inches deep in a block of wood or in old cedar posts. Leave some weeds since their roots give structure to the soil, which helps maintain biomass. Mulch within reason. Mulching conserves water, inhibits unwanted weeds, and as it breaks down it provides important nutrients for the soil, but keep in mind that it's difficult for ground-nesting bees to burrow through it.

Honeybees require water to make honey and to cool their hive. Having a constant source of water will keep them out of the public swimming pool or your neighbor's dog bowl. It's best to provide a shallow dish with an edge or floating corks they can stand on to lean in to drink so they don't drown. A fountain that overflows onto mossy ground is a particularly good, safe way for them to get water. Hummingbirds need lots of water, often drinking up to five times their weight in fluids. They are also fastidious and like to bathe often, so provide a birdbath or self-contained little fountain for them. Butterflies also need water in shallow dishes. If you put sand in the bottom of the dish, they can "puddle" in it, their way of absorbing minerals.

Resist the temptation for a grass lawn; it uses too much water and is useless to pollinators. A little patch of wooly thyme can satisfy the desire for a swath of green. It's soft to walk on, uses little water, and bees love it.

If you have the space, plant fruit and nut trees. Honeybees go crazy for orange blossoms and apple blossoms. They're also essential for pollinating persimmon, plum, pear, peach, apricot, nectarine, quince, pomegranate, cherry, loquat, avocado, pluot, kumquat, and almonds. For large, juicy fruit, keep fruit trees well-pruned and their centers open to create channels of sunlight that can reach all the fruit.

WE NEED ALL THE POLLINATORS WE CAN GET

It's remarkable how much fruit even a single tree can yield if properly pollinated, so be prepared. Get out the pie tins and mason jars. Give fruit to your neighbors or trade apples for apricots. Give surplus to a food bank; there are even people who'll come harvest extra fruit from residential trees and disperse it throughout a network of homeless shelters.

Even a small garden can produce an amazing amount of food. A hundred square feet can yield enough vegetables for a small family for half a year, especially if well planned with early crops followed by late crops. Planting flowers that bees like between rows of vegetables will give even better yields.

Growing our own food is a skill we should all have, not only for disaster preparedness, but because it's nourishing both physically and psychologically. Fruits and vegetables freshly picked have immediate nutritious impact, while their grocery store counterparts suffer vitamin depletion from being transported. Rediscovering the earth as our food source is vital to our psyches as we reconnect to the dormant skill of growing our own food. During World Wars I and II, people were encouraged to plant vegetable gardens to supplement the wartime food supply, and these "Victory Gardens" not only produced nearly forty percent of all fruits and vegetables consumed, but boosted the morale of home gardeners, empowering people to feed themselves and contribute to a larger cause.

There are many creative ways to make the most of a compact space. Instead of letting a squash plant sprawl over precious space in a garden bed, train it to climb an arched arbor and walk under dangling zucchinis instead of roses. Vegetables such as tomatoes, hot and sweet peppers, radishes, lettuce and eggplants do well in containers. Cucumbers, beans, sweet potatoes, peas or strawberries can be grown in a hanging basket in an otherwise unused corner. A sunny garage wall is a perfect place for a fruit tree espalier.

This medieval technique of training a tree to spread two-dimensionally against a wall instead of taking up space and shading much of a yard, can yield as much, if not more, fruit than an untrained tree. Along fences, let peas, beans and any other climbers go crazy crawling up trellises.

Honeybees inspire us to work together in harmony for the good of the whole. Join neighbors over a shovel and a spade in one of the many community gardens taking root in the Bay Area as the urban gardening movement gathers momentum. Besides helping bees and other pollinators, gardens let us reclaim our power from agribusiness, make use of grey water, reduce the carbon footprint of our present food system and provide a place to recycle fruit and vegetable peelings for compost. Perhaps these community gardens have beehives, but if not, the bees will gratefully find all that's been planted. From the front of San Francisco's City Hall turned into a massive food garden several years ago...to Oakland's community garden program where plots are parceled out to residents of all cultures and ages...to Berkeley's garden organizations promoting urban land stewardship... to Richmond's reclamation of land destroyed and abandoned by industry and left to crime, now turned into community gardens...to Marin's weekly Saturday exchanges of excess produce from nearby gardens, people are growing not only food but communities.

8
BEEKEEPERS' FAVORITE RECIPES

"Well," said Pooh, "what I like best—" and then he had to stop and think. Because although Eating Honey was a very good thing to do, there was a moment just before you began to eat it which was better than when you were, but he didn't know what it was called.
 - AA Milne on behalf of Winnie the Pooh

BEEKEEPERS' FAVORITE RECIPES

Cooking with honey instead of sugar increases nutritional value, although high heat destroys some of the quality of the honey. Since honey tastes sweeter than sugar, the general rule when substituting honey is use one part honey to replace 1 ¼ parts sugar. In addition, reduce the total amount of other liquids by ¼ cup for each cup of honey used. Take into account the floral source of the honey since some of its flavor will come through.

When using honey instead of sugar, beat the mixture longer and more energetically. Add a pinch of baking soda for each cup of honey to counteract its slight acidity. Lower the baking temperature by 25 degrees. Honey absorbs moisture, so replacing sugar with honey results in food that remains moist longer. Batter made with honey crisps and browns faster than that made with sugar, so it's great for glazing baked and roasted foods. Also keep in mind that honey will create a firmer, heavier texture.

When measuring honey, coat the measuring cup with vegetable oil first, and the honey will slide right out without leaving any behind.

Honey works well in marinades for chicken, duck,

pork chops or ribs. Because it burns relatively quickly, the marinade can be wiped off before the dish goes in the oven and poured back on when the food is half cooked. This will give the meat a beautiful glazed finish. It's a natural preservative, so it's excellent for pickles and sauces.

Honey is delicious on fruit salads or in smoothies. It can be used as a flavoring for ice cream, but it freezes at a lower temperature than sugar. Honey goes beautifully with yogurt or cheese.

> **Warning! Honey is Not for Babies!**
>
> Raw honey is a natural, healthy food but should NOT be fed to babies under a year old. Although honey doesn't support bacteria, it can carry C. botulinum spores. An infant, with its immature digestive system and undeveloped immune system, is highly susceptible to botulism which can be deadly if not recognized immediately.

Chef Foster, The Fairmont San Francisco

Tamarind-Honey Glaze

This recipe is great for fish, poultry and grilled meat, can be kept for 7 days in the refrigerator.

Serving: 6

4 oz tamarind paste
2 oz local honey
2 oz fresh orange juice
1 Tbsp. chopped cilantro

Preparation:
For the glaze, in a sauce pot add honey, orange juice and tamarind paste, bring to a boil and reduce until it coats the back of a spoon. Remove from heat, add chopped cilantro.

Velvet & Sweet Pea's Purrfumery

Greek Yogurt and Honey

My family and I practically lived on this dish when we were in Greece last summer. It's healthy enough to eat for breakfast and decadent enough to eat for dessert!

1 cup Fage or other Greek yogurt (*Greek yogurt is a rich, thick yogurt that has been strained to remove the whey*)

1 cup fresh fruit, cut into bite-sized pieces (*I like to vary this depending on what's in season – raspberries and peaches in the summer, pears and fresh figs in the fall*)

1-3 tablespoons honey (*if your honey has become solid, simply let it sit in the sun until it becomes liquid again, or set it in a dish of warm water*)

Spread the yogurt in a thick layer on a large dinner plate. Layer the fruit over the yogurt. Drizzle everything with honey. I usually use about a tablespoon, but in Greece they use two or three times that amount, so go crazy!

Makes one serving.

Honeyed Feta with Olives

I can't recall now where I got the inspiration for this dish, but it has been a favorite, both at home and as a party contribution ever since I started keeping bees. The flavors and textures–salty and sweet, crusty and gooey–make a pretty irresistible combination.

½ pound Greek or Bulgarian feta
1 cup olives (*I like mixed Mediterranean olives*)
¼ cup olive oil
1 tsp dried oregano
2-3 Tbsp honey

Preheat oven to 325 degrees.

Put the entire block of feta in an oven-proof container. I have some great ceramic dishes that go from the oven to the table for a beautiful presentation.

Arrange the olives around the feta, and pour the olive oil over both the olives and the cheese. Sprinkle the whole dish generously with dried oregano, preferably Greek oregano. Bake in the oven for 15-20 minutes, until the feta is warmed through.

Remove from oven, place honey in a dollop atop the feta, and let it melt and spread out across the dish. Serve with a crusty baguette (the Cheese Board makes a great one!).

Rose Honey

As a perfumer, flowers and plants are one of my great passions, and they find their way into every part of my life. Honey itself is already the essence of flowers, of course, but this recipe takes honey over the top by infusing it with the scent and delicate flavor of fresh roses.

1 cup of densely packed rose petals (*use petals from the most pungent, most intensely fragrant roses you can find (unsprayed of course, not commercially grown roses!)*
2 cups honey

Use the rose petals only, no other parts of the flower. Grind them in a mortar and pestle until they become a paste with some liquid. This should take only a few minutes. You might have to do a handful at a time depending on how big your mortar is.

Add the paste and liquid to the honey. The petals will color the honey so I like to use rich, deep red for a rosy tint. Let the mixture sit for 2 weeks in a sealed jar. Some people strain out the pieces of petal after this, but this is not necessary.

Once the honey is ready, and if you can resist just spooning it into your mouth, it's gorgeous on fresh fruit, or on a piece of bread, and divine on cheese.

BEEKEEPERS' FAVORITE RECIPES

Marshall's Farm Honey

Mrs. Marshall's Honeycomb & Blue Cheese Plate

This is the simplest way to WOW your guests or hosts. Serve this as either an appetizer or dessert.

Buy some honeycomb from Marshall's Farm. About one or two square inches of comb per guest should be enough. The plate can be prepared many different ways.

1. I like to put a chunk of blue cheese on a platter next to the chunk of honeycomb. I surround the cheese and comb with an assortment of crackers, baguette slices, apple slices and pear slices when pears are in season. Let your guests serve themselves and make the combinations of their choice.

2. Make individual servings, arrange them on a platter surrounding a decorative hunk of comb and a wedge of cheese.

Although this preparation works well with many cheeses strong and mild, I recommend the following cheeses for this dish:

Point Reyes Blue Cheese
Cowgirl's Mount Tam
Spring Hill Cheddar
Spring Hill Dry Jack
Stilton
Gorgonzola
Manchego

Mrs. Marshall's Honey Oatmeal Raisin Coconut Chocolate Chip Cookies

Makes about 4 dozen cookies

½ pound (2 sticks) butter, softened
1 cup Marshall's Farm Bay Area Blend Wildflower Honey
   (*You may substitute the honey variety, but the taste will change*)
½ cup granulated sugar
2 large eggs
1 tsp vanilla
1 cup coconut flour (we use Bob's Red Mill Coconut Flour)
½ cup all-purpose flour
1 tsp baking soda
1 tsp cinnamon
½ tsp salt
2 ½ cups old fashioned uncooked oats
1 ½ cups shredded coconut
1 cup raisins
1 cup chocolate chips

1. Heat oven to 350 degrees
2. Beat together butter, sugar, honey, eggs, vanilla, baking soda, cinnamon and salt until creamy. This can be done by hand.
3. Add flours and stir until blended.
4. Add oats, shredded coconut, raisins and chocolate chips and blend.
5. Drop by rounded tablespoons onto greased or ungreased cookie sheet.
6. Place cookie sheet on top slot of the oven.
7. Bake for 15 minutes or until golden brown.
8. Cool down.

Honey cookies will remain moist and chewy.

Steve Gentry

Salad Dressing Trick

I have a trick that I tell people at the farmers' market. If you like tossed green salads with a vinaigrette dressing try this: approximate the amount of honey that you would put in your vinaigrette if it was sugar, and just convert it, mix up the same ingredients, but don't put the honey in the vinaigrette. Hold back the greens. Dry them and drizzle the honey directly on the leaf, and after the honey's stuck to the leaf, pour your vinaigrette into it and toss it. Not only can you change the flavor, but the way it hits your palate is totally different. It's the same ingredients, but the taste is different, because you're getting the vinegar and the spices before you're getting the sweet. You can make up two salads. One has the honey stuck to the leaf, and the other one doesn't have it, and it will taste like two different dressings.

Because you get the honey at the end, flavors have after-flavors in your mouth. You can change honeys. You can go from star thistle to dark honey to light honey to vegetable honey, and if you develop your palate, you can taste the difference in the honeys after you eat the salad, and as you're eating the salad. There is a difference between those kinds of honey, and you'll get it. You won't get it if you mix it directly, but you'll get it on the leaf if you put it directly on the leaf.

The Melissa Garden

Honey Oat Bars

This recipe is adapted from the Farm Journal Country Cookbook, where it is called Favorite Honey Bars. We make it with 100% organic ingredients.

Makes: 36 small squares or bars

Preheat oven: 350 degrees

Cream together until light and fluffy in a large bowl:
½ cup butter
½ cup sugar
½ cup honey

Add egg and blend:
1 egg, well beaten
Add these dry ingredients and mix well:
⅔ cup whole wheat pastry flour
½ tsp baking soda
½ tsp baking powder
¼ tso salt

Stir in:
1 cup quick cooking rolled oats
1 cup flaked coconut
1 tsp vanilla
1 cup chopped walnuts
1 cup chocolate chips

Spread in large oiled baking pan, such as a 9 x 13 rectangle, or 10 ½ by 15 pan. Bake at 350 degrees for 20-25 minutes. Cool, and then cut into bars or small squares.

The Melissa Garden Honey Bran Muffins

Makes: 2 dozen medium or 15 large muffins

Preheat oven: 400 degrees

Mix together in a large bowl:
1 cup bran flakes (see below – recipe calls for 2 ½ cups total)
1 cup raisins (or substitute chopped dates)
1 cup boiling water
⅓ cup brown sugar, packed
Let sit until cool.

Add each of the following, one at a time, and beat after each addition:
½ cup vegetable oil, such as sunflower or safflower
⅔ cup honey
2 eggs
2 cups buttermilk
1½ cups additional bran flakes

Mix these three ingredients together and stir in:
2 ½ cups whole wheat pastry flour
2 ½ tsp baking soda
½ tsp salt (high quality such as Celtic sea salt)

Optional: Add 1 cup chopped walnuts, etc.

Pour into oiled muffin pans, or muffin pans with paper liners. Bake 20 minutes for medium-sized muffins, slightly longer for large muffins. Cool several minutes before trying to remove from the pan.

Note: This batter can be stored in the fridge for a week and brought to room temperature, for freshly baked muffins in small batches. Fill any empty cups in the muffin pans with hot water.

Greek Tahinomelo

This nourishing spread is popular with Greek beekeepers. Blend the proportions of 60% honey with 40% sesame tahini. For example, to make 2 cups (16 ounces total) use 9.6 ounces honey and 6.4 ounces tahini. You can weigh and measure, or just estimate, as this is a very forgiving recipe. Spread in a thin layer on a dinner plate, then garnish with 1/2 cup chopped pistachios. Serve with pita bread, crackers, or sliced apples.

Greek Pastele (Sesame Bars)

2 cups sesame seeds
1 ¼ cups honey

Preheat oven to 400 degrees. Put sesame seeds in a heavy skillet (that can also be used stove-top), then toast in the oven for about 10 minutes. Remove from oven and place skillet over low heat. Add the honey, stirring. Slowly bring to a firm ball stage (drop a small amount into a cup of water and ice) or about 250 to 256 degrees on a candy thermometer. This stage will take six to eight minutes total cooking time. Pour the mixture onto a large cookie sheet, spreading with a wooden spoon to about 1/8-inch thick. Cool completely, and then break into chunks. Store in zip-lock bags or an airtight container.

The Pollen Princesses

Lemonade

5 - 6 lemons
½ cup sugar
½ cup honey
1 cup water
4 - 5 cups water (to taste)

Cut the lemons in half and juice them to make about 1 cup of lemon juice. Place the juiced lemon halves in a medium sauce pan with ½ cup of sugar and 1 cup of water. Bring to a simmer. Strain the lemon halves out of the simple syrup and add the honey stirring to mix well. Allow the mixture to cool completely. Dilute the mixture with 4-5 cups of cold water.

It's nice to add some lavender water, rose water, raspberries or blueberries.

The Author's Favorite

I'm not a beekeeper but I love honey! This is from Golden Blossom Honey which started in Northern California almost 100 years ago.

Baklava *(yields approx. 40 pieces)*

2 cups walnuts, coarsely chopped
10 Tbsp butter, melted
⅓ cup honey
½ tsp cinnamon
10 sheets of phyllo dough, defrosted
½ cup honey to drizzle on top

Preheat oven to 425°. Butter a 9"x13" baking dish.

Place walnuts in a medium bowl. Stir in 5 Tbsp melted butter, ⅓ cup honey and cinnamon. Brush the tops of five sheets of phyllo with 2 Tbsp melted butter and layer them in the prepared baking pan. (Don't worry if sheets tear apart).

Spread walnuts evenly on top. Brush the tops of remaining five phyllo sheets with 2 Tbsp butter. Place on top of filling. Fold in overhanging phyllo sheets and brush top thoroughly with remaining 1 Tbsp of butter, being sure to cover out to edges with butter.

With a sharp knife, gently slice baklava on the diagonal into 1-1/2 inch strips. Turn pan, slice again on the diagonal, forming diamond shapes.

Bake in center of oven for 15-20 minutes, or until golden and crisp.

While baklava is baking, heat ½ cup honey in a pan to warm. When finished baking, drizzle warm honey over top. Cool.

RESOURCES

The bee is more honored than other animals, not because she labors, but because she labors for others.
 - Saint John Chrysostom

What Honeybees Like and Best Nourishes Them

(Partial list from the Melissa Garden. The complete list can be found on www.themelissagarden.com)

<u>Top Five</u>
Borage
Echium
Goldenrod
Melissa (Lemon Balm)
Phacelia

<u>Others</u>
Agastache (Tutti Frutti, Rupestris, Apricot Sunrise)
Angelica
Aster (Lady In Black, Little Carlow)
Barberry
Black Locust
Blue Sea Holly
Ceanothus (Glorie de Versailles, Anchor Bay, Hearst)
Chaste Tree
Clover (White Sweet and Yellow Sweet)
Coffee berry
Coltsfoot
Coriander
Cornflower
Cosmos
Elderberry
Euonymus
Fireweed
Fuchsia (California selections, cultivars 'Catalina,' 'Chaparral Silver,' 'Schieffelins Choice,' many others) California buckwheat
Gaillardia (Oranges and Lemons)
Germander Evergreen

Globe Thistle (Blue Glow)
Goldenrod (California, Fireworks Eastern)
Gum Plant
Hawthorne
Hazelnut
Heather
Helenium
Horehound
Lavender (Goodwin Creek Gray, Grosso, Spanish)
Licorice mint
Linaria
Linden
Manzanita
Marjorum
Milkweed
Mint (Russian River, Coyote Mint Rangy, Catmint)
Mock orange
Oak
Oregano (Betty Rollins, Herenhausen, Kent Beauty, Greek)
Penstemon (Margarita BOP)
Poppy (California, Shirley, Greek, Morocco)
Rosemary
Rudbeckia (Goldstum)
Sage ((Russian, White, Brandegee, Black, Grape Scented, Sonoma, Bog
Salvia (Purple Rain)
Scabiosa (Pale Yellow
Sedum (Autumn Joy)
Skullcap (Pink Texas)
Sneezeweed Long
Spider Flower
Sticky Monkey Flower
Strawberry tree

Sugar bush
Sunflower (Hairy, Giant)
Tarweed
Thyme (Dot Wells Common, Red Creeping)
Tower of Jewels
Tulips (old species)
Valerian
Verbena
Veronica
Western redbud
Wild Rose
Willow
Yarrow (Sonoma Coast, Apricot Sunrise)

US Department of Agriculture list of plants honeybees pollinate

Fruits and Nuts
Almonds
Apples
Apricots
Avocadoes
Blueberries
Boysenberries
Cantaloupe
Cherries
Citrus
Cranberries
Grapes
Honeydew
Kiwifruit
Loganberries
Macadamia nuts
Nectarines
Olives
Peaches
Pears
Plums/Prunes
Raspberries
Strawberries
Watermelon

Vegetables
Asparagus
Broccoli
Carrots
Cauliflower
Celery
Cucumbers
Onions
Pumpkins
Squash

Field Crops
Alfalfa Hay
Alfalfa Seed
Clover
Cotton Lint
Cotton Seed
Legume Seed
Peanuts
Rapeseed
Soybeans
Sugar Beets
Sunflowers

Beekeepers

David Eichorn
Swarm removal in the East Bay; classes in beekeeping;
Phone: 510-524-9473,
Cell: 510-778-0587
larkhorn@att.net

Laurie Stern
Velvet & Sweet Pea's Purrfumery
www.purrfumery.com
510.528.8040
My vision for my perfumes is to capture the romance of the "golden era" of perfume through romantic scents and gorgeous packaging, and then to blend all this with a modern sensitivity to organics, health, and ethics. At the heart of each Velvet and Sweet Pea perfume is always the profound sense of awe and wonder that I hold for the natural world.

Pat Gibbons, Floral Designer
www.patgibbonsfloral.com

The Melissa Garden
www.themelissagarden.com
The Melissa Garden offers monthly tours, tours by invitation; classes on what to plant for honeybees; workshops on apiculture of the 21st century, with a holistic approach to all elements of living with bees, including information on alternative hives; opportunities to learn about apitherapy, the therapeutic use of products of the hive; and artistic and cultural activities inspired by the honeybees.

Michael Thiele, Apiculturist
www.gaiabees.com
gaiabees@gmail.com
707-540-5072
Alternative bee hives, setting up individual apiaries, seminars, presentations

The "Haengekorb" is made out of rye straw and has nine, half moon shaped arched, movable frames. Comb is built naturally and can be almost 2 feet deep.

Marshall's Farm Honey
Helene & Spencer Marshall
159 Lombard Road
American Canyon CA 94503
www.MarshallsFarmHoney.com
Main 707-556-8088/800-624-4637
Orders: 707-320-3141
Cell: 415-720-4443
helene@marshallshoney.com
Producers of local honey. Seasonal farm tours.

Marin Bee Company
www.marinbeecompany.com
415-235-6424
Marin Bee Company is a green company with a conscience. Our mission is to actively help the environment by repopulating honeybees as they struggle to survive. From installing beehives in home, corporate and community

gardens, to offering adopt-a-hive programs, workshops and beekeeping supplies and free advice.

Steve Gentry
www.stevesbees.org
steve@stevesbees.org
925-254-8063
Find Steve and his products (honey, wax, pollen) at farmers markets in Orinda, Walnut Creek, Moraga, and San Ramon. Steve also sells his honey in several stores (found on his website).

Mauro Correa
www.maurocorrea.com

Tom Manger
www.Beelining.org

The Pollen Princesses
www.etsy.com/shop/PollenPrincesses
Pure Noe Valley specialty wildflower honey from the heart of San Francisco. Gathered from bees kept free of antibiotics.

The Great Sunflower Project
www.greatsunflower.org
Sign up and plant your sunflower. Observe it, record the data on line. The data you collect will shed light on how to help pollinators.

Northern California Beekeeping Clubs

Alameda County Beekeepers Association
510- 531-9423

Contra Costa County Mount Diablo Beekeepers Association
925-458-3900
www.diablobees.org

Marin County Beekeepers Association
www.marincountybeekeepers.org

Sacramento County Beekeepers Association
916-451-2337

San Francisco County Beekeepers Association
415-826-5672
www.sfbee.org

San Francisco Urban Beekeeping Group
www.meetup.com/SFBeeks/

San Mateo County Beekeeper's Guild
650-780-9470 eves
info@SanMateoBee.org

Sonoma County Beekeepers Association
707-578-0797
www.sonomabees.org/

Website for
"Backyard Beekeepers of the Bay Area"

www.backyardbeekeepersbayarea.com